CHAPTER ONE:
When God was a Woman
Act one Scene One: Beginning

Typical Living room,The old man is setting in his recliner, drink in hand, the camera zooms in as He speaks " Long time ago I read a Book Titled When God was a Woman, Great Book, It explained that Everything in Creation did come from a Female, Well, You say She did not do it by Herself Somewhere there has to be a Male to plant His seed, Yes it takes two to Tangle, A Male God and a Female Goddess, If you look back in time during the Time Jesus Christ was alive yes There was a Male God and a Female Goddess as Equal. We know the Romans Called Their God, Jupiter, Their Goddess was Juno. The Greeks called Their God Zeus and Their Goddess was Hera. The Egyptians called their God Osiris and Their Goddess was Isis. Now Two thousand Years later we, as a Society decided to not Honor a Female at All. We have this Illusion of a Male God, A New Male Son of God and another Male we simply call The Holy Spirit. So Who is this third Male Entity? Nobody wants to tell me, they say well they are all One. Ok, If they are all One then why is it a Trinity? If they are all One then who is on the right side of God Intercedding on our Behalf? As a Christian, I hope My Jesus is there putting in a Good word for me on my Judgement day. So that Explains to me there are Two Separate Entities. The only other Male is Lucifer the Real First born Son, Created Long before this World was created." The Ghost Camera Shows Everything, Behind the Scenes, mistakes, and Parts that will Later be edited, gone thru, shortened to make into a Movie. The Camera Scans the Audience, they are in the Largest Auditorium in the city, Thousands of People came from all around to see and Hear the Old man Speak. The camera scans the vast audience, they were Talking among themselves, waiting on the One dog and Pony show to start. The Old man walks out on the Stage, He walks up to the Microphone, takes it off the Podium and Reaches his hand out and a Chair slides over to him. No One else see's this, Not Even the Camera Crew, all They See is a Old man Talking to Him self, They Laugh among themselves, they were told to Follow the Old man and record everything, This is what they were paid to do. The Old Man was Very Rich, Thru The Years, He Has Been Fair to People and they have Made Him Rich Beyond His Means. He wanted To Share some of His crazy Motivational Stories, That is Why the Film Crew are Here.To Follow him around, film his Seminars and go back to His Mansion and Listen to all the Stories of Elusive Treasures and this New book all about Fingerprints., but now He has proof that what we were taught is all wrong. What gives Him the Right? Time will tell. Yes, there is another Camera crew from the Local Tv station, They to want to Record his talk and a Lot of Preachers from local Church's are Here, Listening to What He has to say. The Old Man Holds His Hand up for People to Listen and They do, He talks: " I am Melvin Abercrombie, for those who do Not Know me,Yes I have been Searching for God all My Life.I knew there has to be a Female some where in this creation Process, so I was also Looking for Her too. I have gone to Various Church's and Different Religions trying to Find out Whose God is Better then the Other God. I have read the Different Versions of the Holy Bible,the Lost books of the Bible, the Dead Sea Scrolls,the Nag Hammadi, The Buddah, the Koran, and others, Who Is Right? Who Is wrong? Who gets to decide? I have written many Books,if you ever read any of my books, then you will see I talk a lot about the same Topic,Only thru Repitition will we finally absorb the Truth. I believe there are Ten main Topics that people do not want to change. We,as a Society, have advanced in every Technology except Religion,we are still in the Cave man mode. People do not want to know the Truth,they are afraid,Why? You have the Right to ask Questions and Demand answers. If you read any of My books you will see I like to tell a lot of stories, I want you, the reader or watcher of ths Movie to get your money worth.I grew up as a Christian Baptist, We were Taught there is a 3 Male Trinity Consisting of a Male God, Yahweh, a New Male Son of God, Jesus and another Entity called a Male Holy Spirit. For the last ten Years I wrote all my books wanting this third entity to not be a Male entity but a Female, so to my way of thinking, the Holy Spirit is actually the Goddess, the Wife of God, Yes the Shekhinah, so This I wrote in all my books, I asked God for this Understanding Heart to Help Me understand what I need to do during this lifetime, Thru my Ego and Pride, I wanted to Continue were the Da Vinci Code left off, Yes Dan Brown did write a Great Book, Over 50 Million People bought and read His Book and Tom Hanks made a Great Actor in the Movie, which also was a great Block buster Movie, So that tells me there are a Lot of People who are Interested in all this Religion. So Now what do we do? Were is the Continuation? Were is the Church we go to? It don't make sense to teach all this then just stop? I wanted this Ideal to keep gong yes we have the Momentum lets create a Church Ministry were Now we can all go to Worship this Male God and this Female Goddess as Equal. I call it Avalon Ministry, Yes The Real Trinity A Real same God, the New Jesus Christ and a Female Wife of God as Equal as this Holy Spirit and a Real Trinity. People are not satisfied or happy with what they are being Taught, Yes Jesus was Married, Yes Jesus Did have Children, Yes the Religions did not like what He was Telling so they had to kill Him, to Silence Him. Now again We do know that a Third of the Angels, Led by Lucifer, was Cast out of Heaven, Why? Could Lucifer, Being the Real First born Son, Knowing He was the Only Person who Has the Right to Someday Ruling over something and then knowing that the Father would Never Die, get a Third of His Brothers and Sisters to Join Him in this Rebellion, then God Getting Mad and casting them out of Heaven? So Where did these Fallen Angels go to? Could God Realize that they only wanted something to Rule over, so God Created this World, Created Adam and Eve and stand back to let these Fallen Angels Rule some-thing? Yes, does this make sense? We do know, after a While, God Did look down and saw all the Evil and He said He wished He Never Created This World, so He Tried to Destroy this By a Flood? Now stop a Moment, If God Looked Down then Is God in a Flying Saucer or spaceship? Is God in this other Dimension we want to think of as Heaven? So we know that God,after a while, Did look down and saw this Evil, so who was Running things? We know Jesus was not born yet, There was no Christian Trinity, who created All this Evil that God looked down and saw? The only Person who has this Power is The Real First Born Son. Yes we, as Christians were Taught that Our Jesus Christ is the ONLY Son of our God,Hello Wake up. If Jesus Christ is the ONLY Son of God then Who Created Lucifer? Who Created All these Angels, Who Created Adam and Eve? and all these billions of People created long before Jesus was Born? The Symbol of a Male is a Triangle with one point up showing the Male Anatomy, The Symbol of a Female is a Upside down Triangle with one pont down showing the Female Anatomy, This has been a Symbol for Thousands of Years, Long before Jesus was Born. If you Take these two Triangles or Trinity and Intertwine them together does this show the Six pointed star of David or the Original Symbol of the Hebrew People? Yes, The Hebrew were the Chosen People, Long before the New Jewish Religion was Created. So If a Threee Pointed Triangle or Trinity Represents a Male Anatomy are there Three Males in this Creation Process? Yes, You have the Original Male God, Yahweh as the Father Creator, The Real First born Son, Lucifer, Created Long before Jesus was born and Long Before Adam, Eve and This World was Created and then of Course, Adam, The First Mortal Human Male Created so did these Original Hebrew People Teach the three Males In their Religion? Now what about the Female? If God Did have a Wife, and Many Cultures, Civilizations did Believe that then does God Have a Wife, Yes, You call Her Shekhinah, Queen of Heaven, The First Born Daughter is Auriel, You call Her, Mother Earth and of Course Eve, The First Born Mortal Human, Then Now we have a Female Triangle or Trinty all Created Long Before Our Jesus Christ was Born, So to me, The Original Hebrew Did Teach this Equality, Just like the Egyptians having Osiris and Isis and the Egyptian Pharoah's Daughter who took Moses in as a Baby and Brought Him up Knowing the Equality. So Now we as Christians do Not Want this Female in our Trinity or Triangle we do not want two Triangles or Trinity's so we Eliminate Lucifer out of this Creation Process.   Yes, You have good and Evil inside you, What better Teacher to teach you evil then Lucifer? You do have a Choice,Feed Good you become good, Feed Evil You become evil The Different Religions around when Jesus was alive did Under-stand and Teach this Male God and this Female Goddess as Equal, We will Talk about this again and again,All these People alive when Jesus was alive they all had a Fingerprint." Short break.The Old man speaks again:" I like to tell a Story. Say you have two Men, One goes to Church, Pays His ten Percent, is Faithful all His life, does no wrong, lives a good Long Life then He dies and You were Taught He gets to go to Heaven Forever and Ever. He only gets one chance at this game you call Life. He Gets Married has Children, has a Nice Typical Job, then He dies, Gets to go thru the Pearly Gates, Gets to walk the Streets of Gold and Gets a Mansion and Lives Happily forever and ever. This is what you were Taught, Must Be right? Now you have another Person, Born Mean as Hell, Kills, Steals, does Horrible things all His Lifetime, Right before He dies, He calls in a Preacher, confesses His Sins, Says the 3 Magic Words "God Forgive Me" and Now because of What you were Taught, He is saved By Grace and He did say the 3 Magic Words "God Forgive me" then He too Gets to go thru the same Pearly gates,the Same Streets of Gold and He too Gets a Mansion Forever and Ever?? Does that Seem Fair?? You sacrificed All Your Life and this Guy gets the Same Reward? Can you come up with at Least a Hundred Bad things He has Done? Can you come up with at Least a Hundred Good deeds this good man has done? Is there a Hundred Shades of Red color between the good man and this Evil Man? Does Not Matter He has said the 3 Magic Words, "God Forgive Me", He gets the same treatment you do, You were Taught there are only Two Choices, Either you get to go to Heaven Forever or you Burn in Hell Forever. Thats it?? Only Two Choices. No, You cry out, God That is Not Fair, So Now you have the right to Question, what you were Taught, Could your Parents and Family maybe Wrong? So you start looking, and you realize there are Many Wisdoms and Knowledge out there. So our Church Ministry we call Avalon, We Believe, Yes there is a Male God and a Female Goddess as Equal, there is a Dual Triangle Trinity, We, as many Cultures in many different Language, Did worship a Male Type Entity God and a Female Type Entity Goddess as Equal,This was 2,000 years ago while our Jesus was alive, History does prove this, some say its only a Myth and that is why its called Mythology but if its only a Myth then how can you go to Egypt, Greece and Rome Italy today and still see the Remnants, the Statues, the writings on the walls etc? So Now You do have a Choice. Now we also know that everything has to have a Opposite like Up and down, Forward and Backward, Male and Female etc so now the Opposite of Good has to be Evil, so did God Create Evil? Someone did, so if the Original first born Son was Lucifer and He was Evil does that make sense? Can you, a Creator destroy all Evil? What would the World be like if God did destroy all Evil? If there was Only good, You had No Choice would you, after a While get Bored? You as a Christian, Were Taught you die and get to go to Heaven forever and ever so after a while will that get Boring? Or you burn in Hell forever and ever, after a While will that get boring too? We have to have Good and Evil, No, Its inside you, now how much good or Evil you have is up to how you were Created and Taught. All you know is what you were Taught. They can Only Teach you what they were Taught. You can not go to a Doctor and tell them to cut the Evil out, again there is Evil and good in every person, the one power you feed the most will be what you become, the worse word in the world is the word OR, we are taught that it is either this OR that, if we take the word OR out of everything and put the word AND in its place then we do not have division we have both, which is what we actually do have, you do not have one OR the other, you have one AND the other, One does not completely go away you have both, you don't have just good or Evil you have both. So Now If Lucifer was the First born Son and Auriel was the First born Daughter, You can call them what ever name you want to, I just was Taught that the Original First born Son was called Lucifer, so to me that makes sense. Now we do know from reading the Bible that there were many, many more Sons and Daughters born, Because the Bible tells Us that a Third of the Angels, Led By Lucifer, had a Rebellion and were cast out of Heaven. Remember this all Happened Long before this world was created and Long before Adam and Eve were Created,Long before our Jesus was born, so if Lucifer Led the Rebellion, then He must of Known that He would Have to be the First born Son, the Only one who had the Power to Rebell, everyone knows when a King dies then the First born will take over the Kingdom right? Of course, the problem is the King never dies, so what does the First born do? He gets a third of His Brothers and sisters to join Him and they have a Rebellion. So Now our God Cast them out of Heaven. So were did they Go? So now our Creator God and Goddess decide to create a World to give these Rebellious Children something to Rule over, does that make sense? So now Adam and Eve were created in OUR Image, in the Image of US, which tells me at that time there was a Male Entity type God, in Hebrew, He is called Yahweh and a Female type

Entity Goddess, in Hebrew, She is called Shekhinah. So you say Why Hebrew? According to all Books I read, the Hebrew were the Chosen People and in the Beginning there was One Religion, One Church and one Language, Adam and Eve spoke the Hebrew Language, God and Goddess spoke the Hebrew Language. So Adam and Eve were created to give these Fallen Angels something to rule over, so God stood back and watched. We all know what happened, the Angels became what we now call Demons, after a while God looked down and saw all the Evil and He said He wished He Never created mankind, so He tried to destroy the World by having a flood." stop for a short Break End of Chapter one

Chapter Two: Goliath
Scene Two Act Two:

the Old man continues talking: " Now also remember Genesis Chapter six that says the Sons of God looked down and saw the Daughters of men were fair and they took them wives and their were Giants created. So was this Before the Flood or after the Flood? Now after the flood the only ones who survived were Noah and His Family Right? But how do you explain the Giants of David and Goliath? Did the Demons,the Fallen Angels, still go into Humans and create more Giants? If a third of the Arch Angels were cast out and become Demons, so does that mean there are still Two thirds called Angels? Some believe the Aliens, the race of Annunaki came to Earth, which could be these same Fallen Angels? These space Aliens may have come here in their Flying Saucers or space vehicles and maybe they were large, compared to regular Human beings? Has anyone else thought of the Annunaki as the Fallen Angels? Even the Idea that our God, Goddess and All Angels were the Space Aliens from another Planet? Could what we call Heaven be that other planet they were from? To me that would make sense, So my Question is How did the Sons of God look down? Were they in a Flying saucer or something up in the Air? How did they get here if everything on Earth was destroyed by the Flood except Noah, His wife His three sons, Shem, Ham and Japeth and their Wives? None of them were Giants, so did these Giants Fly here with wings or a Space ship? We believe Moses was Taught these stories and He is the Author of Genesis, Now Who Raised Moses? We know the Pharoah's Daughter took the Baby Moses and raised Him up, so could Moses see First hand these Giants Helping Build these Pyramids? What do they gain by coming down here and Helping build these Giant Pyramids unless as Beacons for other space craft to be able to see were they were? We know the Pyramids could be seen from a large distance in space. A lot of people do believe some Aliens from another planet have visited us thru out time, even the Mayan in

South America and old Mexico and Roswell New Mexico. Thru out History, its safe to say different Aliens, from different planets have visited us, not all are Little greem men with big eyes. Yes, Some could have been Giants in size. Now everyone knows the Story of David and Goliath. Most of you, thru the years, in a Church of some type, heard the story of a Small David, who Challenges the Mighty Goliath. Understand Goliath was the Biggest, Meanest, Toughest of all Giants. He earned the Right to be Their Leader. Yes, He fought many Battles and won because of His Mighty size, Strength and His Armor He wore.. Yes, You do not win in a Battle unless you have a lot of good armor to protect you from arrows and swords. David knew this from a Distant He could see that Goliath was a Mighty big Giant and with His Armor it would be hard to Win but David knew everyone has their weakness and thru the armor Goliath had to see his Opponent and His Eyes were His Weak Point only a Rock with enough force right between the Eyes would Stumble him for a Moment and a Moment was what He needed. When David walked out to fight Goliath Everyone was Laughing. Goliath looked down and saw a Crazy boy. Laughing, He said give it your best shot, He thought the Rock would only bounce off His armor, He was Hit with many tough Swords and axe and was wounded several times He was not afraid of this little man. What Goliath did not Understand was that David Had the Will of God Behind Him and with the Courage David Aimed His One chance Rock and Hit The Giant Right Between the Eyes. This temporary Knocked the Giant down only for a Moment. If David would have walked away bragging about what he would have done then Eventually Goliath would have Gotten up, sore yes, but now mad as Hell and killed David, so while Goliath was down, David had to Kill Goliath at the Only weak point in His armor, sword right in the Eye Socket the only vulnerable spot with a small sword. As Goliath layed there dead, to show all the other Giants that He, David, Killed the Mighty Goliath, He removed the Helmet and Cut off His Head and Put it on a Tall Pole so that all the other Giants could see their Leader, they Recognize, was Dead and this man David, did kill Him. they knew small as He was He must have Power from the Gods and they did not want to fight Him. Everyone knows that David became a Great Ruler but He also did some bad things and we will talk about them thru out this book. David was Never a Christian. Jesus Christ was not even born during this time. They did Teach the Old dual Trinity, None of the New Testament was even written during His Reign. A lot of People believe He spoke Hebrew language and kept the Hebrew Laws of Keeping the 7th day Saturday Sabbath and Moses Laws of Certain foods being Clean and Unclean, the Levitical Kosher food laws, so it was easy to assume David, or any of His Hebrew People did not eat Pork, catfish lobster shrimp or other unclean foods,Yes, He was under the Hebrew Law. Now also remember Abraham had two sons Issac and Ismael We Believe Ismael became the islam Religion around 400 A.D.after Jesus was Killed, and Issac had two sons Jacob and Esau. We all know Jacob's Name was Changed to Israel and had 12 sons who became the 12 tribes of Israel which started the Jewish Religion. Now before all this they were Hebrew. We know the Islam people called their God Allah and the Hebrew called their God Yahweh, was this just a Language issue? We know many civilizations had different names for this God, Egyptians called Him Osiris, Romans called Him Jupiter, Greeks called Him Zeus, Vikings and Teutonics called Him Odin and Celtics called Him Cerrunos, its the Same God, just different Languages, Different customs, Who is right? who is wrong? who gets to decide? Now back to Goliath. We know different Cultures tell the Story and the Islam is the same. The Koran and other Books they Teach Now, Today,tell you the Story of David and Goliath as part of their History. Their Version says They are the Little David, Islam, and Isis and Guess who the Big Goliath is Now ? Yes,the Big and Mighty United States of America, we are the Mean Ugly Giant Goliath. We no longer Keep the True 7th day Saturday Sabbath, We follow Lucifer, the Sun God and keep the 1st day of the week,We have so many different Christian Religions, we are "Scattered and Confused". We tell everyone its ok, to Now worship a Male God, a New Male Son of God and another Male Holy Spirit, so now Christianity has Three Male Gods and they call them a Trinity not a Triangle, and Now its ok to worship all three Male Gods on Sunday the 1st day of the week and Sunday Night starting the 2nd day of the week. Todays Christians also teach they are no longer Under God's Levitical Kosher unclean/clean Food Law but now you can eat all kinds of Scavenger foods because some Radical named Paul said Now its ok. No wonder they call Us Infidels, No wonder they want to Chop our heads off,Thats what you do with a Ugly Giant, We, as the United States of America, are now betrayed as Goliath. Do you blame them? Why would One God go to all the Trouble, not once but twice tell His Chosen People to obey Him? They had to do certain Laws, Keep the Ten Commandments, Keep the Clean /Unclean Levitical food laws, but No, we have to accept the Teachings of Paul who saw a Spirit, a Blinding light, He thought was a Angel, Yes It was a Angel called Lucifer, Who is still Laughing at how stupid and Gullible the so called Christians are." stop for a Break end of chapter Two

Chapter Three: Re-Incarnation

Act three Scene Three: the Old man speaks: "The next topic is Resurrection versus Re-Incarnation. What is the difference between Re-Incarnation and Resurrection? Have you ever looked at a Dictionary at their meaning of each word? To me Re-

Incarnation means you live so many years, You Do Experience All The Things you Need to Experience during this Lifetime, In your Physical Human temporary flesh and blood, mortal body and Then you die. Your Spirit/Soul Is Judged and You go into a New, Different Re-Incarnated, New Temporary flesh and blood, mortal body, with a New Skin Color, New Hair color, New Culture to Experience but with the same Fingerprint, same Dna, Why? Because you can not possibly Experience all the different things you want or need to in only one lifetime, so our God and Goddess gave us the Opportunity to go into a New Re-Incarnated body to Experience different things Maybe one life you get to be White, the next life maybe Black or Oriental or Spanish, one life maybe a Male another life maybe a Female, Could this be why some People Think they are Gay or Lesbian? Some say I am a Woman trapped in a Mans body or I am a Man trapped in a Womans Body?Could they have been a Male in a Past life and Now they are a Female and sometimes they have a Partial Recall of a Past life? Now what is the Difference between Resurrection? Its Not the same thing. If you did not get to experience All of what you needed during this lifetime, do to a accidental death before your time, Then Yes you are Judged and then you get to go into a new Resurrected body, maybe with the same skin color,same eye color, same fingerprint, same culture and same dna to finish that Experience, Just two words Meaning almost the same thing. I have these Dreams about my Past life, I believe I did not get to Experience All the things I needed to Experience so Now I am going Back again In this Life to Finish it. I was Born December 29, 1949, so that means my Spirit Soul had to Leave my Previous Body Before that date. I was a Preacher in my past life, probably a Baptist ,Teaching this False 3 Male Trinity on Sunday. I was Happily Married, with a Teenage Son and Daughter. I worked as a Carpenter, Framing Houses for a Living. I just bought a Brand New 1949 Red Ford Coupe, It had the Flathead motor with Dual Exhaust and three speed Transmission, That was cool, at the Time. Near by there was a Prison, and sometimes I would do Church service there for the Prisoners. One Saturday Night, My Wife was Cooking fried Chicken,I was watching sports on TV. Three Black Guys Broke out of Prison,They Found some big sticks, they could use as clubs and Came to our House.They Barged in the Front door and caught us off guard. They said they were Not going to hurt us, so they Tied us up. They found my Guns in the Closet,I had a 45 Pistol, a Shot gun and a deer Rifle 30/30.they took them,my billfold and Her purse, They smelled the Fried Chicken, then Helped themselves. One said He Recognized me as the Preacher. They decided to Rape my Wife and Daughter, I started Hollering, so they gagged all of Us,then one said, They will Recognize Us and we will get the Electric Chair,All I wanted to do was get Free,and Kill them,Yes I was a Preacher, telling others to Turn the cheek,Forgive those who done you wrong, Even Jesus said Right Before He died to Forgive those, I could not do that, I wanted Vengenance,The Black Guy with the 45 Pistol said out loud, Dead Men tell no tales as He Shot my Son,Then My Daughter, Then My Wife, Then He pointed it at me and Said Ok Preacher You want to Forgive Us, make your peace before Your God, I wanted to break Free I wanted to Kill all three of them I heard the Gun shot, Felt the Pain as the Bullet went into my Skull. Yes, we were all dead, My Spirit Soul Left my now Dead Body, I could look down and see all four dead Bodies, I still had hate, i wanted to still Strangle them, I tried, but I was Now a Ghost. they all got in the car and I went with them,They Could not see Me, and I guess God allowed this . They got on the Highway and Up ahead was a Road Block, The Sheriff and Police wanted to Check Every car. They each had a Gun and knew they would not go back alive, They speed up and crashed thru the Roadblock, the Police and Sheriff started Firing, my brand new Red 49 ford coupe was Demolished,it turned over on its side and gas poured out I could see all three of them were Wounded but kept on shooting and so did the Sheriff and Police, My spirit got out of the car and I watched as All three got Burned Alive, I could here their agony and crying, but no one would help them, my Spirit was satisfied, My Preaching was All In Vain. I did Not Say, God Forgive them and Let God do the Judgement, Yes, the Shades of Red, I was Very Mad and hateful The Devil Possess Me, I realized that Now I will Stand before this God, And He would Judge me, I wanted another Chance, so Now I am In this Body, Do I have the Same Finger-print? I don't know. I did write another book titled Fingerprint. I grew up in the fifty and sixties, so during that time there was a lot of Hate among the black and White.This was before Martin Luther King came along, The Blacks Lived in one area and the Whites lived in another area,This is part of our past, Now I realize there is Good in all Color, Yes there are some Evil black People, Yes there are some Evil white People. What shade of Red are you on? Can you move up to another level? Just like the Circular staircase, can you take a Step forward or Backward.. Did I go thru a New Re-Incarnation with a New Body or did I go thru a Resurrection? You either get a New Resurrected Body or a New Re-Incarnated Body. All you know is what you were Taught. I was Born in this life,right Now, as a White Male. Yes I do remember some of my past life Experience, or was they some crazy dream? I was taught as a Christian Baptist, because that was what my Parents and Grand parents were Taught. Now you understand why someone born in Japan, for Example, maybe were Taught that their God is a Big, fat, bald, Oriental Guy named Buddah. Who is right? all they know is what they were Taught Do not blame them. So how many lives do you get to live? Does everyone just get one life and we all get to go to Heaven forever? Are their actually Pearly gates and streets of Gold and Jesus going to give everyone a Mansion? Can you Imagine Bilions and Billions of People all Getting a Big Mansion? What will You do in Your Mansion? Can you eat? Drink? Get Married? Have Kids? Will You have a Fingerprint? What about Paul's Writing saying the Oceans and graves will give up the dead and those that are alive will be caught up in this Future Rapture?" He pauses, Drinks a glass of water then continues:" So is grandma up in Heaven right now or is She still in the Ground waiting on a Future Rapture to Come? Again, all you know is what you were Taught. They can only Teach you what they were Taught, does that make sense? Or does Re-Incarnation Make sense. So that means you are living in your Version of Heaven or Hell Right Now. Each Life you are Here to Experience certain Things. You live a Mean, hateful, Killing life and the Next life you realize Karma is a Bitch and now you must go thru a Lifetime of being Crippled, Disease, Handicap, Blind or disabled, so that is your Heaven or Hell. Just like the story in Chapter one Two Men, one living a good life and the other being very mean but at the last minute say the three magic words "God Forgive me" You were taught that both get to go to the same Heaven or Hell does that seem fair?" He Pauses. looks at the Audience,see if anyone says anything,then Continues:" Now if you accept the idealogy of Re-incarnation then Yes, God can forgive you, but you still are accountable, still are responsible. Yes every knee shall bow and you will be judged, so maybe Now you get to go into a New Body.You see Innocent babies born Crippled, handicap, disease and your heart goes out and wonder why would a kind, loving, merciful God allow this and Now You understand, they have to Experience these things. Maybe they did not do anything bad maybe they just need to Experience being born blind or crippled as part of their Evolutionary Experience, now does that make sense? How do you know what its like to be born blind, Crippled or handicapped? Unless you actually go thru that particular Experience? Remember the Holy Bible is a Bunch of Individual People Telling you Their "Version" of What they think actually did Happen, that is Why its called a "Version", Matthew is Telling you His Version of What He thinks, In His Mind, actually Did Happen. Luke is telling you, His Version, of What He thinks, actually Did happen,Yes, Each Person has Their Opinion. The Original "Version" has been changed a Hundred times, so what you are reading today is only part of what the Original Authors wanted to say,also Remember two things Jesus did say, One "You have Eyes but do not see and you have ears but do not Hear" is the first, over and over Yeshua tells anyone Listening, the second is "If you

Love Me, Keep My Commandments" again over and over Yeshua, the Ha Mashiach tells anyone who hears these simple parts of a Puzzle. I believe in Equal rights, Not Just between a Male and a Female but Equality for Everyone. Some are born Rich, others are born Poor Why? Every Person has to Experience all the Different things. I can Write a Book about being White and Rich but until you actually go out and Experience this for Yourself then its not the same. I can write a Book about being Black and Poor but then you will say How can I write a Book about being Black and Poor when its Obvious I am a White Person? Yes During this Lifetime I may be Born as a White Person. I am a Very Old Spirit Soul, who has lived Many Lifetimes,Yes I do Believe in Re-Incarnation. Yes, I do believe in Resurrection They are Different, The Holy Bible says that Jesus was the Word and the Word was there from the Beginning, so was Jesus a Re-Incarnation of Adam? We Know Adam and Eve did Have a Fingerprint Why? Was this God's Way of Identification come Judgement day? Your Physical, Mortal Temporary, Flesh and Blood Body Does die and Does That Fingerprint also Die to? Can you get that same Fingerprint in a New Re-Incarnated Body or a New Resurrected Body so God Could Identify Who you are? We know the Physical, flesh and Blood Adam did live a Long time, then his Physical Mortal, Temporary, Body did die, could He have been Re-Incarnated into another person? Eventually maybe into Noah? then maybe Abraham or maybe Moses and finally thru Elijah, then The Jesus christ? Jesus did say Who do People say I am? one said Some say You are Elijah. How can Jesus Be Elijah, who lived before with a Different face, different Fingerprint or was it? Yes Of Course Even Jesus Christ Himself did Die a Material Death, or did He? Pilate New the Seventh day Saturday Sabbath was about to Be here so He Instructed the Soldier to Make sure the Ones on the Cross were Dead, If Not They were Instructed to Break their Legs to speed up the Death,By not having their Legs to stand on this would Hasten their inevitable death.People,including Doubting Thomas, saw the Roman Soldier stick the Spear in the Side of Christ to see if He was Dead. Jesus did not move, so the Roman Soldier assumed He was already Dead, so He Did Not Have to Break His Legs. Now Here we have Two Theories, One the Person putting the Sponge on the Stick gave Jesus a Elixir to Simulate His Death and Their "Version" was Jesus Never Died, He Assimilated the Death and was Brought back alive. The Other Theory is that Our Jesus Christ Did Experience the Pain of Death and Really Did Die, Just like Lazarius and others did. He did lay in the Tomb for three days and His Mother, The Virgin Mary and His Wife, Mary Magdalene did Go see Him and Realized He was brought back alive thru Resurrection. Yes Jesus did not Finish what He Needed to Experience so God Could Have Brought Him back alive.THey also Knew if He walked outside, People would see Him and Recognize Him, They would go tell the Romans He was still alive and Have to go thru that again, We also knew there was Roman Soldiers guarding the Tomb to Make Sure Nothing happened, We all Know in Different Versions the Soldiers were Drugged or went to sleep and when they woke they found the Rock rolled away and the Tomb was Empty,so they Convinced Jesus to Let them Shave Him and Cut His Hair. I remember a Long time ago, I too had a Beard and Long hair. One day I went into the Bathroom, Looked in the Mirror Did Not Like what I saw. Cut my Hair and Shaved My Beard off. I was Having a Hard time Getting a Job, People Do Judge a Book by looking at the Cover, so when I walked out of the Bathroom, my own Kids did not Recognize me, they Started crying, Even My Dog started Barking at Me, My Wife came in to see what was the Matter and Surprised, She too had to look twice. I reasurred all of them and My Voice, they could see another Me. Could this be why Thomas is called Doubting Thomas? Think about it for a Moment. Could this be Really What Happened? Thomas was on the Road, walking with this Guy, Who said He was The Christ and Thomas saw the Roman Soldier Stick the Spear in His side, so He did Confront This man, Calling Him self the Christ and Jesus Did Show Him the Hole in His side and this is the Story You heard about the Doubting Thomas. Now the Big Question is How Long did this Jesus Christ Really Live? Everyone Read the Book about the Da Vinci code and saw the Movie.over fifity Million copies of the Book were sold, Why? Because Dan Brown brought up this Female side of God, Yes Jesus Christ was Married, But Now were is the Church you actually Go to? what Next? Yes Jesus Christ Did Have Children,Yes to be a Jewish Rabbi you had to be married and Blessed with a Son as part of the Rabbi Require-ments, You don't just walk into a Jewish synagogue and start reading the Torah unless you have the Breastplate with the Credentials showing you are authorized just like a General has the Star symbol. The Jewish Law says all Rabbi's Have to be Upstanding in their Community, Married and Blessed with at least one Son to be able to go to School and they were amazed at how Young He was Teaching from the Torah.The Holy Bible is very clear showing that He did do these things. Jesus Christ did Leave that town under Roman Rule to get away from the Jewish People who are the Ones who wanted Him dead, Did Jesus Travel To other Countries? Yes, Did He Have More Children? Yes did His Children have Children? Yes, Can the Bloodline of Jesus still be here Today? Yes the same Dna Were is this Church Mnistry that keeps this Experience going? We want to Make Avalon Your Church Ministry would it be so bad if you had at least One Avalon Ministry in every City, Every State, All over the World? Would that be so Bad? Yes you will still have your other

Christian Religions, Yes your Buddah, Hindu, Jewish, Islam and others. Would it be so bad to teach Re-Incarnation and Resurrection as a Viable alternative? So Now Can other people be Resurrected? Yes,Of Course, say for Example you are a Blonde, Blue Eyed White Male, you have a Certain Dna and Fingerprint. You were Born as a Mortal, Flesh and Blood Temporary Human so you can Experience certain things during this lifetime. Now say you live twenty years and a Accident does Happen, a Car runs out in front of you and Kills you. Did you get to Experience all the Things you wanted to or needed to during that lifetime? No, of Course not. We know there are accidents all the time, People die before their time, Airplane crashes, Tornados,Tsunami or other Flash floods or accidents always happen.So your Temporary flesh and blood mortal body did die, this white, blonde hair, blue eyed, twenty year old body does die. You came from a Female and it goes back to a Female. You call Her Auriel, Mother Earth. Your Spirit/soul is Judged,Yes "Every knee shall bow and Every Tongue shall Confess". God and Goddess Decide you did not get to Experience everything you needed in that one lifetime, so your Spirit/Soul goes back into a New Resurrected Baby and Get to Finish the Things you need to do. Yes You are Born again and come out as a New Resurrected White Baby Boy, with the Same Blonde Hair, and Blue eyes ,the same Dna, and Now, Do you have the Same Fingerprint? We, as a Society, decide when someone dies, that we Delete the Fingerprint from our Computer base. A Day will come, and we will figure maybe what I am saying does make sense, so we will put all these Deceased Fingerprints in a Archive Computer base, and see Twenty years from now, if anyone is born with the same Finger-print.. So Now, How many times do you get to be Resurrected? Once? Twice? Three times? Or maybe as many times it takes to get you to Experience All the Things you need to Experience During that Lifetime. Sometimes People Can get everything done in only one lifetime, Yes they live to a Ripe old age of a Hundred and Experience all the Things they Needed and are Ready to Go into a New ReIncarnated Body, Maybe they were Blonde hair, White skin and Blue eyed during one lifetime, so now they Did Experience that, so now, if they did Live a Good Life then they get to Experience another skin color, or another Eye color or another Profession, Can you be a Doctor, Lawyer, Electrician, Plumber, Architect, Engineer, and or five hundred other Skills in only one lifetime? If you did bad things during one life then are Judged, can you go into another Life and have certain Disease's or Problems? Maybe this is why you see some People Rich, others Poor. Some living Long Healthy, Disease free life while others seem to be attracted to Problems, The saying "You Reap what you sow" does that Mean anything? Now you kind of Understand what

Resurrection Means, anyway, its just my definition and Now Re-Incarnation Happens when you Experience all the Things you need to do in that Resurrected Body and You are Ready to Move Up to a New Re-Incarnated Body, so Can you keep the same Fingerprint? A time will tell in the future, when we decide, maybe we can put all these fingerprints in a storage file and maybe see in another life, a person does get to keep their same fingerprint, life after life, this would be one way to know who you are each life? Remember there are Billions and Trillions of different people living at any one point in time, so go back thousands of years with all these different fingerprints? So having the same fingerprint in each life would make sense and a time in the future, we could actually say wow, That person was another person in a previous life? We, as a society, have not advanced enough to imagine this yet, so for know each life ends and so does the Fingerprint, again, we, as a Society have advanced in every Technology except Religion. We want to Cling to this Old Cave Man Mentality, you only get one life, You die and you get to go to Heaven forever and ever, or if you were a Bad boy or a Bad Girl then you get to Go to Hell forever and ever. Then you wonder why we are so "Scattered and Confused" Ok, I say, that is enough lecture for one Night I want to thank everyone for being here, Yes, I will have more Lectures we all Need to think about all the things i have said ,Yes ,Read my Books, Yes, ask Questions, Thank you." End of Lecture at Building scene End of Chapter Three

Chapter Four: Kosher Food Law

Act Four Scene four:Home in His Mansion, Camera ready Scene is his Living Room setting in His Favorite Chair, Fresh cup of coffee in hand the old man speaks again " I Studied the Holy Bible, the Lost books of the Bible, the Nag Hammadi, the Dead Sea Scrolls, the Koran and most every Religion trying to find God and the Goddess. Who is right? Who is wrong, who gets to decide. I do Know that our Creator's Plan was, there are certain Animals, birds and Fish that were created as Scavengers to make this World work right, this makes sense, God told us what we should eat and what we should not eat, but did we obey? No, Just like Lucifer, we to became Rebellious and with the help of Lucifer and the Third of the Demons living on this earth, we as a Society, decided we do not have to obey God, so now we are definitely Scattered and confused and will remain so until we accept the truths that were written, time and time again. Mainly by Moses in the Levitical Kosher food Laws, which desribe in detail, which are called Clean and which are called Unclean, then we wonder why we have so many Diseases and do not realize, its all because of the germs and bacteria from eating unclean scavenger foods." He Paused, Took a Drink of Coffee,then Continued "We have Atheist who do not believe in a

God at all and some of them realize yes, There are certain foods that do have a Bacteria or germ, and if eaten then that Germ or Bacteria could spread and cause a Cancer or other Disease, so its not just the Religious People, God put this in the Holy Bible for everyone to see, that is just part of the Creation Process.Also Remember the Holy Bible was not written until Moses grew up and wrote the First five books so Now the question is what was the Holy Bible before this time frame? The Egyptians and other Civilizatins did Exist and most was Verbal, Just like the Pharaoh's Daughter Taught the Young Moses, they Worshipped a Male God, they may have called Osiris and a Female Goddess they Did call Isis, you can go to Egypt today and still see the Remnants and Statues of the Goddess Isis . The point is why did God create clean food and unclean food in the first place? Would God just only make clean food,make it easier for us? When you look at the Big Picture, then you see the World is constantly changing, things grow and die out, Humans, Animals, Birds and fish all go thru this Cycle of Birth and death. Once they die, then they slowly go back to Auriel, First born Daughter,Mother Earth thru being Decompose, yes from ashes to ashes, dust to dust.So Now the Question Was God a Female in the Beginning? Everything came from a Female at Birth and Everything will go back to a Female at death, so certain Animals, Birds and Fishes have to be created to help this circle of Cycles Yes, these are created to eat these dead species, so Now they are called Unclean, because they have Bacteria and other germs, Everyone knows a Pig is a Scavenger and to eat Pork you have to Cook the meat to a Certain Temperature, to kill the germs and Bacteria, does this just go away and Disappear? No, The Bacteria and Germs are still there, hope-fully, they are all dead, but they still go into your body and bloodstream and sometimes, if the Bacteria did not all die, could that Bacteria become a Cancer cell? What is a Cancer Cell? a Fat Cell? a Bacteria Cell, a Germ Cell? what is the Difference? is a Cell a Cell? I remember in school, Science and Biology, we studied different types of Cells and got to look under a Cool Microscope at all the moving stuff, crawling around. Now Imagine that stuff crawling around inside you, going thru your Veins and Arteries, and maybe lodging in a Area and Multiplying? and become a Tumor, or some other Cancer type cell? So if you know pork and other foods do have a Bacteria and you know you have to cook it to a certain Temperature to kill this bacteria and you know if you eat this bacteria, it can multiply in your body, you know this stuff, even if you cook it and hopefully kill this bacteria, it still just don't Disappear, you are still eating this dead bacteria, then why are you that stupid to eat it? Yes there was a Time People were Hungry and they would eat most anything and of course Lucifer is going to tell you that its ok, you killed that bacteria and Now Paul said it was ok to eat scavenger food Now, because we are no longer under that old Law no more. Then we wonder why People call Us Christians Infidels and its Not just one group of so called Christians we can not agree on anything so we have over five hundred different types of so called Christian Churchs and a whole lot of different Denominations and Tenets of Faith and Different Doctrinal Statement and Lucifer is Laughing His Butt off and God is Shaking His Head thinking, I tried to show you the Truth, in the Holy Bible but you Choose to Not Believe, Just Thinking??" end of Chapter 4

Chapter Five 7th Day Sabbath

Scene five Act Five Now in His Den in His Mansion walking around showing all the Different rooms and Talking the same time, the film crew gladly follows Him around,The old man Speaks " In this Lecture you will see I have Ten Basic Tenets of My Faith, You have seen so far, The Goddess, as the Wife of God, Yes the Shekhinah, so did She Create the Male God? Did She Marry Him? We know Lucifer as the Real first born Son of God and our Goddess. We want to think as males, that in the beginning a Male God Created all this by His self. Yes the Male does plant a seed but it takes a Female to do the Creating so could there actually be a Female in the beginning or maybe they both were there as a Duality?,So The idea as When God was a Woman, Does that make sense? the story of Goliath then, we talked about Re-Incarnation or Resurrection, Yes, I will repeat my self over and over, Remember when you were in school that is how you remember things and next, was the Levitical Kosher food Clean?Unclean food Laws, so Now the next topic is, the true 7th day of rest. The Bible makes it clear, not once but Twice, God Put it in His Ten Commandments, that He did Create this World in 6 Days and He did Rest on the 7th day. The Hebrew, Jewish, some Christians and others still follow this Commandment Number four but you say, well we are No longer under the Law. Ok, lets talk about that One, what about the Commandment that says "Thou shalt not kill or we under that Commandment? Yes, of course you can't go around killing people, then what about the Commandment that says "Thou shalt not Steal" are we under that Law? of course, you can not go around stealing things, so you say you get to pick which one of these Ten Commandments you want to be under, and which ones you do not want to be under? Again, you say well Paul said its ok to do this or its ok to do that, are you a Follower of Paul or of Jesus? Remember Jesus did live about 33 years during that time, He Never Worshipped on Sunday, Neither did most of the other Disciples, they were all Good Jewish/Hebrew type People. Only in 313ad, the Roman Emperor Constantine changed the Law, Why? Some People were wanting to take off work Sunday, the 1st day of the week, because their Jesus arose from the Grave on Sunday, Even in His death, He Obeyed the 7th day Saturday Sabbath and waited till the 1st day of the week to Arose. So People were taking off Saturday and Sunday and Constantine saw there was Not Much work getting done, so He decided to make it a Official Law that Sunday is the 1st day of the week and the Roman Holiday. This started the Roman Catholic Church, So for almost three hundred Years, everyone still kept the 7th day Saturday Sabbath as God did Command, but you say does it matter? Yes, God Created this World in six days and He Rested on the 7th day, it does not matter if you are Jewish, Hebrew, Islam,Hindu or Christian, its the same God, and this same God made it very clear what day you should rest. The point is, God made it very Clear, His People, those who wanted to Obey Him, Should rest on the 7th day, which is Friday night and all day Saturday, as the true 7th day Sabbath, Those who want to follow Lucifer the Sun God and the God of this World would Worship the Sun God on Sunday the 1st day of the week. The funny thing is, if you go to Church Sunday Night, you are actually worshipping on the 2nd day of the week, Look at any Dictionary, They do not lie, Sunday is the 1st day of the week, all ways has been , Monday is the 2nd day of the week, look at your calender, then wonder why you are having so much problems, no wonder you are "Scattered and Confused". I know I said the same thing over and over in this book, and my other books and the reason is only thru repitition will you remember things, remember there are Ten Secrets in this book, some will be obvious, others you have to seek, so they are not just labeled, yes the first five I did that, so now the last few you may have to read this twice to catch the Secrets, some will find eleven or twelve, others will only see seven or eight, then you are not ready yet. Sometimes what you think you need and what God actually knows you are ready for, maybe different. I learned that the hard way, I thought if God would only give me Millions of Dollars, I could help a Lot of People, so I was Mad because Millions of People did not just go out and buy my books, I mean these secrets could help make the World a Better Place, but then Finally I realized that You maybe need to go thru Your Trials and Tribulations, If someone was always there to help you out, then you never get to Experience Failure or being broke or going thru these Obstacles, which hopefully will make you better. What don't kill you will make you better, Does only living one life then get to go to Heaven or Hell Forever make sense? Did you get to Experience all the Wonderful things you like to Experience in only one life? Can there be a Hundred Different shades or Levels of Good? can there be at least a Hundred different shades or Levels of Evil? Yes you are Judged then you get to go back at a Different Shade or Level and Experience some of the Different things you did not get to

Experience in your past life." The Film crew and I decide to stop for a Lunch break the camera Crew can keep on Filming as we talk and eat, mingle with all the people involved in the Filming yes, It does take a few People to make a Movie. End of Chapter five

Chapter Six Why was Jesus Killed?

Scene six Act Six: Now outside, its a Beautiful day, back yard next to the Swimming pool, with the Rock waterfall, everyone relaxed, having drinks, casual, laid back, The Old man likes his Hurricane Drink, so the Bartender makes his and he takes a sip, sets down in a Lounge chair, as the Camera Zooms in, The old man speaks " Does anyone ever wonder why Jesus Christ was Killed in the First place? The Roman Leader Pilate found no fault in Him, and washed His hands of the Matter. The Jewish Rabbi's had to Kill Jesus to Silence Him. Jesus spoke in Parables, Why? some of His Teachings were a Secret. Most People did not Understand, Only those ready to accept His Real Teachings, understood the Real Meaning hidden inside the Parables. The things He was saying they did not approve of, remember they had a big scam going on, making a lot of Money, what ever sin you commited, no problem just find a innocent animal, bring it to the Rabbi and with a Little money, the Rabbi would pray over it and you were Forgiven. Now, also remember, there was no Welfare, No food stamps, no section8 housing, so how do you take care of the homeless, the needy, the crippled, the Blind? You get people to fall for this lie, and go find a Calf or lamb, and the Rabbi's used this to feed the Needy, to them it made sense. Some Rabbi's got very rich off this, so now this upstart named Yeshua comes along telling the Truth. The Three Wise men Knew this was the Real Messiah, The Jewish People thought the New Ha Mashiach would solve all their Problems so to them this New Guy was good but He did not solve all their Problems, They Did Not Realize they Needed to Experience these things, They wanted someone to take away all these problems so to them this Guy was not their Messiah and His Teachings were Good, to good . So they had to kill him to silence Him. You see Jesus did not die on the cross for your sins, Jesus died to do away with the sacrificial Law. Why should a innocent animal die for something you did? The innocent animal did nothing wrong, so Jesus did not die for your sins, you are accountable. Why is there a Judgement day if you are already forgiven? Church's today tell you that you are saved by Grace and Jesus Died on the Cross for your sins, NO Jesus Christ Yeshua Christus Died on the Cross to do away with the Sacrificial Law only. Why is there a Judgement day? You don't get to Tell God, the Preacher told you that you were saved by Grace, then why is there a Judgement Day if you are already saved by Grace? When Your Physical Mortal Body does Die and your Spirit Soul is Judged, Yes you will Stand before God,

Yes Every Knee shall Bow and Every Tongue shall Confess, You don't get to Tell God that You are saved By Grace, Why is there a Judgement day if you are already saved by Grace? I try to get People to at least think about different topics, yes, one minute I talk about one thing, then another I go off on another subject Why? Sometimes I feel my mind is going twenty miles per hour and my body is only going three miles per hour. Does that make sense? Yes, my books are different. Would it be so Bad to have One Big Religion were everyone agree's? Yes there is a Male God,Now what ever name you want to call this God is Up to You. We all speak a Different Language, so we have Different Belief's but its still the same Male God,What ever name you want to Call Him.. The Same with the Female Side of God, She Has many Names, Its ok to Be Involved in Avalon Ministry and Still call Her By What ever name makes you Happy, If you say a Prayer then you are Calling upon that God or Goddess. Another Group calls themselves Christian Wicca, They Do Mean well, She is Trying to Join the Female Goddess Wicca Religion, with the Christian Religion which is Great. Now What about all the Other Religions? What about Islam Do you create Islam Wicca? or Jewish Wicca or Hindu Wicca? See My Point, Only when we Combine All the Religions and Call Upon our God and Our Goddess thru Prayer will they Hear Us. In Wicca they go thru three Initiations, I know, I went thru them myself,Yes we had a High Priestess, Who Oversaw everything and you cast your circle, back then it was with the opening to the East, because the Sun did rise from the east and that was the way We were Taught.,To me,that does not make sense, the Guardian of the East is Raphael, He is the Air, Do we Honor Him First? I always thought the Opening should be from the North,that way Auriel, our Mother Earth Would get the Respect first,Of Course You would enter the Circle, call upon your God and Goddess first then face North and Call upon the Guardian of the North, Which was at the Beginning,She was the First born Daughter. If You Go back in time, before Adam and Eve, then we Know there was a Male God, I call Him Yahweh and He did have a Wife, I call Her Shekhinah, for over 2,000 Years Society and Church's Have Hidden Her . I was Taught that the chosen People were the Hebrew People, so to Me, I would Choose the Hebrew Name of our God and Goddess. They Had Children, you call them Angels or Arch Angels. The First born Son was Called Lucifer and the First born Daughter was Auriel,She is Mother Earth. We Know There was a Rebellion and a Third of the Arch Angels,Led By Lucifer, were Cast out of Heaven.Were did These Fallen Angels go? Were are they Now? Could there be Demons among us Now? Of Course Lucifer was Cast to the Sun,He Is the First born and He Is the Light.. Auriel Did Not take a part of this Rebellion, She was Given this Earth and We Call Her

Mother Earth. God and The Goddess Created Mortal Humans to give Lucifer and the Fallen Angels something to Rule over. God Stood back and Watched to see What they would do,After a While God said He Wished He would Have Never Created Mankind, Why? He Saw all the Evil that Lucifer and the Fallen Angels Created and He tried to Destroy it with a Flood. These are Things You already Know.   Now When we Combine the Three Initiations of Wicca to the Male Creator Religions what will Happen? I Like to See a Male High Priest and a Female High Priestess as Equal. They Can Be Husband and Wife or What the Coven or Church Chooses. Each Avalon Ministry Will Have as its Members a Lot of Different People with Different Religious Backgrounds, the Common Thread is the Willingness to Agree Upon a Equal Male Creator God and a Female Creator Goddess, We choose Yahweh as the Male Creator Name and Shekhinah as Our Female Goddess Creator Name, Why? Once again, I believe the Chosen People were Called the Hebrew People, This is Not The Circumsised Jewish People,The Original Hebrew were Not Circumsised. Adam and All of His Sons were Not Circumsised and all the way down to Noah and His Sons,Shem,Ham and Japeth were Not Circumsised. This was a Clean Issue Brought out by Moses much later, I believe Lucifer told God that He could Convince Gods Chosen People to allow Lucifer to put a Permanent Mark of the Beast on All the Chosen People Males,This mark would be on Their Forehead and anyone could see they Now had the Mark of Lucifer on them. God Believed His chosen People would not fall for that, so God Allowed Lucifer to try and do it. Remember the Male anatomy called the Penis, the top is called the Head, This piece that was butchered and cut off is called the Fore skin,so the Mark on the Fore Head is the Butchering and removing this FORE Skin to permanently Mark You When you change the Original Hebrew Language to Greek, Latin and finally to our English you see the Mark of the Beast is on the Forehead and is a permanent marking showing the 666. Why Did God Put this Foreskin on the Male Anatomy in the First place? To Protect. What you are doing is saying God does not Know what He is doing and I will Butcher my Male Babies because these People allowed it and they actually Allowed Jesus Him self to Be Butchered. Forgive me If I am Wrong. Paul said It does not Matter we are only Temporary Physical Spirit Souls, our Immortal Spirit is Not Circumcised, only the Physical so we are Not doing what God said to do Only what Lucifer, The God of this World wants to Put this Mark of the Beast yes, This 666 on Your Fore Head.So what does the 666 actually Mean? If you realize at one point in time there were only 2,000 People in the whole World, This World was not Created Yet so they were in the Place we call Heaven and If you subtract the Father God and Mother Goddess then you have at one pont in time 1,998 Children,Yes Sons and Daughters you call Angels, so If a Third Led By Lucifer were Involved in this Rebellion then you get the Number 666 as the Number of Sons and Daughters Known as Angels that were cast out of Heaven, So Now they Become what we call Demons, Remember also Lucifer was a Beautiful Cherub after He Convinced Eve to Do Her Temptation then God Changed Him to a Demonic Snake for Defy-ing God Twice.. Now I did go thru the three Initiations of Wicca, Now we will call our Religion Avalon Ministry, so I would Like to Change the Casting of a Circle, which is Temporary and Use a Permanent Full Bubble Circle, Completely surrounding you 24 hours a day, 7 days a week, 365 days a year.You Have the Guardian of the North, in Honor of Auriel,our Mother Earth, Then Go Clockwise to Raphael, the Guardian of the East, Deosil to South, were Michael is the Guardian of the South, and Fire and then go to West,Were the Guardian is Gabriel, and She Rules the Water, then on around Back to the North to Complete the Circle. One Difference is, we Do Call Upon our Goddess and Our God to Come in to Our Circle of Protection. Here we Can Add the Teachings of Christ and Invite Him into the Circle,We Can add the Teachings of Allah and add Him and Mohammed and the Koran to the Circle,We Can add the Hindu and Buddah to the Circle, How do you know what is right unless you understand why other People Believe what they Believe?. So now instead of Casting a Temporary Circle, go into the Circle, say your Request, then close the Circle down. You Keep the Circle or Bubble all over you, to Protect you from Evil,Believe me, If Lucifer see's a chance to enter, He will.,What do you want to learn? Are You Happy with Just Only the Teachings of Jesus? Would the World Be a Little Better If You Incorporate some Buddah,Hindu and Koran Teachings to Your Congregation? Are You Going to Burn in Hell Forever If you Decide to Open your Doors and Let Others Teach you a Little about Their Religions? In the Old Wicca, the Male was Her Consort or During the Sping Festival He Came, Planted His seed, then Lived Thru the Summer and Fall, then Died out during the Winter, that was their Way, Because They Did Not Agree with all the Different Male Dominant Creator Religions. Now in our Church,The Male God Does Not Die out, He Is Equal to the Goddess, Yes He Plants His Seed and The Female in all Creation do the Creating Together, In Balance, Perfect Love Perfect trust. How Many People Here Knows the Eight Words of the Wicca Law?." He Pauses Takes a Drink of Coffee Looks around then Continues "The Wicca Law is Now Our Law of Avalon Ministry and that Eight Words are "And You Harm None Do What You Will". Now How Many People Had to Memorize the Wicca Rede as Part of their Initiation? I Remember back in the Seventies, to Show My Age, I was a Part of a Coven and I went thru the three Initiations. We are a Non Denominational Church Ministry Not a Coven, Avalon Worship's a Male God,Yahweh and a Female Goddess, Shekhinah, as Equal. We Keep a Lot of the Teachings of Wicca and Christianity, also Jewish, Hindu, Budda and Islam, even the Egyptian Teachings. I Did Memorize the Wicca Rede and I want to Incorporate it as Our Law Now, Let Me See if I Memorized it Right "Obey The Wicca Law You Must, In Perfect Love,In Perfect trust. Eight Words, the Wicca Rede Fulfil, And You Harm None,Do What You Will, Least of all thru thy own self Defense it Be, Forever Mind the Rule of Three. Follow this In Mind and Heart.Merry you meet, and Merry you shall Part." Something Close to That. It Needs to be a Requirement for a Person to Go thru a Initiation of Joining our Church, and Being able to Recite the Basic Law of Three. I am Under the Three Fold Law,If I Do Good then My God and Goddess May Bless Me, but If I do Evil, I have seen Up to a Three Fold Curse.It is Our Law. Christians use the Eleven words of Their Law to say the same thing "Do Unto Others as You would Have Then Do Unto You" its the same as our Law of Eight Words "And You Harm None,Do What You Will" are we Under the Ten Command-ments? Yes, You can Not Go out and Kill People Or Steal Things so Yes we are Under God's Law, Jesus Christ Is still Our Teacher, Avalon is still a Christian Church,Jesus Taught us "If You Love Me then Keep My Commandments". What would it Hurt if a Islam Came to Our Church and Studied the Christian and Ethic ways? What If He Taught Us some of the Teachings of the Koran? Would we Be more "Enlightened?" So is Islam,Buddah Hindu and The Jewish Rabbi's Teaching Different? You Have this Illusion, when you die you get to go to Heaven forever, so is the Hindu, Buddah, Islam,Jewish Up there also? What did they Believe before Jesus was Born? Its the Same God and The Teachings are To do good. I would Like Different Speakers from Different Denominations to Join our Ministry and Teach Us The Different Teachings, Not Just Wicca, But Christian, Islam, the Koran the Buddah, the Egyptian Teaching's, and The Hindu and the Lost books,Nag Hammadi and others. There is So Much we as a Church Ministry Need to Learn. I do Have One Rule, We Will Never Pass the Offering Plate around. Yes It does Take a Lot of Money To Make a Church Ministry Work. Each Avalon Church Ministry, at the Entrance Door will Have a Big Wood Box, Bolted to the Floor, with a Lock and a Slot in top saying Thithes, Offerings and Prayer Request. Anyone who feels they want to be a Part of the Ministry, Can Put in their Money, You Will Not Be Judged if You do Not Give Ten Percent. This is something Between you and God/Goddess, The More You Give, the More You get back, its The Law,Yes You Want a Fancy Building, then Some one Has to Pay for it. You Want Air condition and Heat and Lights, Then Someone Has to Pay for it.

You want Music and People to Work at the Church? Then they Expect to Get Paid for their Services, It would be Nice If Everyone Did this for Free, But Reality is, if You want to Be a part of a Ministry It Does Take Money" I Hold My Hand up to show My Coffee Cup is empty,short break, The Camera Crew was told To Stay with him for the Next Ten days, Each Day He Would Reveal One of His Many Treasures Telling the World about this Male God and Female Goddess as Equal,the way it was in the Beginning. But His Idea Was Only One Treasure at a time, Give the People Time to Absorb this,Yes He had the Biggest Ocean Front Property and Every Day He Loved to Walk on His Private Beach early In the Morning and Sometimes Watching the Sun Go Down, Yes He was Very Rich and Old, He Wanted to Film this so Others Could Benefit, The Film Crew Were allowed to Stay as His Guest for the Ten Day's and His Butler's and Maids would Provide for Them, Now With a New Fresh Cup of Coffee, The old man speaks:" When I found the Aladdin Lamp,I realized I only got one wish, What would you wish for? Knowing you only get one wish? Lots of Money? A Long Life? a Healthy, disease free Life? I Think about Asking for my Life Back, Maybe go Back in Time, the Last 6o Plus Years, when He was a Kid, Yes Knowing What He Knows Now Could He Go Back in a Time Machine, But If He Changed One Little Thing would that Change History? He Often Dreamed What Would Life Be Like If He Never got Married, But then He Would Not Have His Beautiful Children and Grandchildren and Marriage was Not all that bad, Yes the Divorce and the Greedy Lawyers trying to Get their Half of the Money The Only One Who Benefits from a Divorce is the Greedy Lawyers. It's a Shame. He Remember His Grandpa Who Always Told Him "A Man Is Only as Good as His Word, When You Can Look a Man In the Eye, Shake His Hand and Give Your Word then That is all You Need" But Now People Lie to You they Steal and Kill for Money,No Money Is Not the Root of Evil, Its How You Obtain it. God Even Told You, He Does Not Want you To Be Poor. Grandpa Was Very Religious, Dad was the Opposite, Yes He was Very Wealthy and Tried Going to Church when I was a Child But the False Preacher's Who Kept saying Give Me Ten Percent of Your Money or You will Burn in Hell Forever Pushed Dad away. So We Quit going to Church. I Looked For God in Various Church's and Religions But Finally Gave Up When Mom Died from Cancer, She Believed God Could of Healed Her, But all Our Money Could Not. Cancer is a Evil Deadly Disease, I Realize Now It's a Bacteria, Just Like anything You Are what you Eat and Mom Smoked and Ate Scavenger food. Doctors Tried to Tell Her to Stop Smoking, But She would Not give It Up, It was To Late for Her, So the Last 30 Years, I quit all Dealings with God, Goddess, All Religions all Church's, Then I Remember Grandpa Telling me about There are

ten Treasure's, That Have Made you Very Successful and Now it's Time to Share these with the World and Now you will Share with this World thru Your Understanding Heart, you will Tell The World these Truths, Many People Will Buy your Book and You Will Title the Book Fingerprint and this will Be the Movie they will Make."
The Seminar was Great the Old man said the same things over and over again, the Camera Crew was Told to Film everything, no matter what,They Could get all the Film back at the Studio and go thru it, Delete all the Scenes they wanted to, and get this down to a One Hour Movie, People would want to see.So Yes, they were paid a great sum of money to follow the old man around and Now He is going back to his Mansion and Tomorrow will start a New Elusive Treasure He calls them. Next Scene.Next day, Its early Morning The Old man gets a fresh Cup of Coffee, sets down in his Living room the Camera crew set up, drink their coffee, everything is Casual, kind of laid back, everyone is Friendly, they have a Job to do and the Old Man has a Message to Share with the World. Now He Talks: "People Look at Themselves Backwards. They Assume they are a Mortal Flesh and Blood Temporary Human Who Happens to Have Somewhere Inside of them a Spirit/Soul. In Reality you are a Immortal Spirit/ Soul who has lived many Life-times, Each Life you get to go into a Temporary Mortal, Flesh and Blood Body so you can get to Experience the Different things you need to Experience during This lifetime, You look around and see Millions and Billions of Mortal Flesh and Blood Humans with different fingerprints All Going thru what they Need to Experience, Sometimes our Paths do cross, Once you realize we All are Here to Experience Different things then you can Not Change this by Writing one Book, They will read this Book and Hopefully Now Understand Yes, Why they are Here and Will Be Better at Under-standing Why,But they still have to go thru that Experience. Remember It took the Spirit World over 40 Years to Explain all this to Me. Here I am Trying to Tell You 40 years of Knowledge, Crammed in a Short Book, Yes, It will Be Over-whelming to some, Others will accept and Realize what All They were doing wrong. What Works for One Person May Not Work for Another. Think about this, If You are a Doctor or Counselor, then You were Trained In School to Help Others. Once You Realize someone Has a Problem then with Your Training you would Tell Them What You Would Do, If You Were Them. The Problem Is, You are Not Them. What works for You May Not Work for Them. What Works for One Person May Not Work for another person. You See We all Have a Different Fingerprint, with A Different Genetic make up, with a Different Dna, Etc. I am a Immortal Spirit/Soul, who Has Lived over 2,000 Years. Some of My Past Lives I do Remember, and I Talked about some of these in Various Books. I am Temporary Stuck in

this Mortal Flesh and Blood, Human Body, So I can Feed, Eat, Drink, Experience the Things I Need to Do, During this Lifetime. Yes, I do Have a Immortal Spirit/Soul, Yes I am What you would Call a Vampire. I do Not Drink Blood, That is All Movie Hype to Protect Us from your Stupidity. I Absorb your Power, Your Energy, Some call Us Physic Vampires, Yes, I can Touch You and Absorb your Energy like a vacuum. I can Draw your Energy, your Power, Just Like a Prostitute will Not Only Take Your Money from You, They Will Take your Lifeforce, your Orgasm and Leave You Drained, Sometimes Smiling and wanting to Come back for More. Not Every one Has a Immortal Spirit/ Soul. Yes, Some are Just here, Just Like Animal, Birds and Fish, Just Here to Live so many Years, Experience What they Need to Experience then they Die. You Came from a Female In this Creation Process and Will Return to a Female. You Call Her "Mother Earth" End of Chapter .Its getting dark another day,yes they all go home for the night tomorrow another Lecture end of chapter Six

Chapter Seven
Circular Staircase
Act Seven Scene Seven

Next day the film crew are once again ready we are in the dining room everyone enjoying breakfast and coffee, once they all finish the old man stands for a moment to let everyone know, lets get this film rolling, the camera guys are ready to film, He sets back down takes another drink of coffee and says "Now It Is Time to Tell a Story. I want to Share some of My Motivational Stories I hinted on a Few already and Each chapter I want to share some of these Stories or what I call Elusive Tresures. I am Here During This LIfetlme to Tell Everyone some Basic Truths, Most You already Know Maybe Just another angle. If You Can Imagine Everyone in The World Millions. Billions,Trillions of People All on this Great Big Circular Staircase," I Pause, Take a Drink of Coffee then go on:"You Look Up and see a Lot of People Higher Up then You, But Now You Under-stand, Maybe they are Older or Know Things you Do Not Know, Maybe You Graduated from High School and Maybe they Have a College Degree, Maybe a Associate or Bachelor Degree, Maybe Way Up there, they Have the Doctor's Degree, You Can Look Down and see There are People Lower Than You, Maybe They Do Not Have Their High School Diploma or They are Younger than you are. You Do Not Know, it But there are a Lot of People On the Same Step You are on, Because You are, Maybe in Texas, They May be In New York, California or Japan?" Again, I Pause take another drink of Coffee then go on" Now You Can

Come Back in Five Years and See That Some People are Still on the Same Step. They Are Not Going Up or Down, But Happy Were they are at, Is this Wrong?" again I pause to Show I am Out of Coffee so I get Up Pour My self another cup, set back down and continue:" So Now You Know maybe another Secret is the Circular Staircase, Its hard to Visualize Millions of People all on a Circular Staircase, But Try to Visualize Me at the Very Top, Yes I was Soaring with the Eagles. I had Everything, The Guy with the Silver spoon or Really a Gold Spoon,. then One Night, I was Out Were I should Not have Been, Yes I was Wild and Crazy Drunk, I Drove My Custom Van Home. I had Money, I could Call My Limo Driver to Drive me Home, It was three o'clock in the Morning and My Stupid Pride said You can do this. My Ego when I am Drunk is a Different Person, I Dozed Off for only a Second, Going 70 mph down the Freeway, I Hit the Edge of a Bridge and the Van Flipped over on its Side. Now You Sober Up Real Fast. You Realize, There are No Brakes and No Steering, You are Still Going down the road 70 mph and Your Van is Flipped over, The Gas Tank is On Your side and Is Naturally Pouring out, and the Van is on Fire. You Try to Open the Passenger door to Climb out, and You Did Not Push it Far Enough, so the Door Comes Back and Knocks You Back into the Van, and The Fire. You Realize then, You are Going to Die, They Say, At the End, Your Whole Life Flashes Before You, Yes that is True. In my moment of Dispair, I cried out, Help me God, I do not want to die. a voice told me to try again,this time I pushed the door open and climbed out, the same voice said Run, and do not look back, I looked anyway. to see my Beautiful custom van Explode,the gas tank did that, Fire shot up 40 feet and Knocked me down, I rolled over, on fire and Tried to put my self out.A truck driver came and with his small Fire extinguisher, He put my clothes out and took me to a Hospital. I had to call my wife to come pick me up. I spent the next three weeks in a VA Hospital recovering from all the Burn, What is the Secret about this? What is the Elusive Treasure Here? I was soaring with Eagles,Yes thru my pride, my ego, I was way up on top of the Circular staircase. I lost Everything, for you see that was the Straw that broke the Camels Back, My Wife left me took our Kids and went home to Her Family, I was stuck in a Hospital for three weeks of agony and Pain. But I feel I needed to Experience these things, again I can Write a Book about all this, But I needed to Experience these things first hand." I Pause for a Moment Get a Fresh Drink in Hand and Continue: " I Like to Tell Motivational Stories, some You Have to Figure out, Could this be one of the Secrets? You Were Told I May Only Reveal One Secret a Day, But then on the Other hand Its My Life,Who Knows I May Not Be around for the next Ten Days, No One Is Promised Tomorrow" The Old man Continues with another story or is it another Secret? This is actually another Elusive tresure Who is Counting? So what happens if I give you more then Ten? Only Those who really Read Every word will Be surprised at all the Elusive Treasure. So Imagine a Early Morning bedroom Scene, The Alarm goes off ,He climb out of bed and heads to the Bathroom. As He reach's around the wall to Turn the Bathroom Light on, He rubs His Chin, thinking I need to Shave.He looks in the Mirror as the Camera Zooms in ,the Black smoke shows the Demon Entering His body as His eyes turn a Glossy Black. He rolls His head around and smiles. He reachs in the Drawer for Scissors and start cutting all His gray hair off, Then He reachs for the shave cream and gob a lot all over His head. He Shaves everything off but His Moustache. Then He takes His Pajamas off, as He opens the Shower curtain, naked He climbs in the shower, closes the curtain, turn the shower on.The Camera goes to a Boxing Arena, a Crowd of People watching a Boxing Match. The Pretty girl in a Bikini walks around instead of Showing round two or Round five, she has a Big card showing five minutes later. Everyone is amused. The Shower stops,the curtain opens, He steps out and grabs a Towel to Dry Off. The camera zooms in and shows all the New Tattoos on His chest and upper arms. His Eyes are still Glossy black, showing the Demon is still Inside of Him. He drops the towel and raises His hands in the air, declaring to all the World, the Power He now has. Two large black Raven wings over 4 ft tall appear on His back, as they start flapping, He rises from the ground. the camera shows His feet are off the ground. Out of no were a lightning bolt appears with a loud thunder, His right wing snaps off," He falls to the ground, naked He rolls into a Ball on the floor, He cries out loud, "Forgive me God, Forgive me Goddess, Forgive me Father, Forgive me Mother." Thru My Pride and Arrogance, my Wing was Broken. He laid on the Floor, Naked sobbing. the camera Zooms in on His naked back showing the Broken wing with blood flowing down His back, the other wing folds up as He sobs uncontrollably.A few Minutes go by then the two black wings disappear, the Blood disappears. He grabs the towel from the floor as He wipes His face He reach's with His left hand, the top of the Bathroom sink to Pull His self up. His hand shapeshifts into a Demonic hand, with long fingernails showing the Entity is still Inside of Him. Then He reach's with His other hand to pull Him self up, and it too shapeshifts into a demonic hand, with long fingernails, only for a moment, so the viewer can see the Entity is still inside of Him, as He pulls Him self up,He dries Him self off with a Towel and Then He notices the Tattoos all over His chest and Upper arms. He grabs a Wash cloth and scrub His chest and arms trying to remove the tattoos, He cries out to no one "Is this the Mark of the Beast?" " Forgive me Father, Forgive me Mother", He sobs to no avail. Finally He puts His underwear and clothes on. He looks in the mirror and the Glossy black eyes disappear, only His normal eyes. He grabs the Hair brush to comb His hair and Then He realize's, He cut all His Hair off. He brushs His moustache and eyebrows, The only hair He has left. As He put His Watch on He notices the time," The Camera Crew will Be here soon". He starts to Reach up to turn the Bathroom light off, He pause's in Mid air. Twirl His Fingers around and the Lights go off. He Knows He Now Has the Power." How do I use It? How do I Control it?" He remembers when He was a Alcoholic, the eight words that Helped Him get over that addiction. "You Control it or,It Will Control You." So Now with this New Power Knowing the Spirit World is watching You Have to follow the Eight words of Mother Earth and they are "And You Harm None,Do What you Will," He ponders the Idea that both of the Important Powers now in His Life have Eight Words. Why Eight? He thinks to Him self, Remem-bering as His Hand Shape-shifted in this Demonic hand with Long Fingernails as He grabbed the edge of the Bathroom sink," are the Fingerprints left, mine or some other Demonic entity?". He has watched enough Movies and real Life to Under stand that if this was a Crime scene then they would dust for finger-prints and Any found would be put in the Data base , Everyone Knows this . He grabs His Coffee cup and takes a drink as the Butler Lets Him Know His Guest Have arrived .They are Unaware of the Ghost Camera, for You see, No One Can see the Ghost Camera, Is it a Ghost? The Presence running the Lone Camera feels to be another Female, Yes Young, You see a Glimpse of Her every once in a While. Now He Has the Power, He can Now see Her More Clearly. the Other Film Crew are Unaware of the Ghost Camera Filming all the Behind the Scenes activity. They Set Up In The Living room He always wanted to get into the Movie Business and that was what these Four Young People chose. You Have to Start out doing Minor Task learning the Ropes, same with any trade or business. you can not just go up there and tell them you want your High School diploma or Bachelor Degree You have to take the Time and earn it. Just Like in the Army you Can't just go up there and say you want to be a General, again you have to Earn it. He wonders about this New Power He has, Will This Demon appear again? Will His Hands or other parts of His Body Shape shift into this Demonic creature? What about The Raven Wings one was Broken, Yes He felt the Pain coursing thru His Body as if You broke a Leg, the Excruciating pain He did Feel, was it my Imagination? He felt the Blood Pouring down His back as He curled up on the Floor, was all this His Imagination? Yes the Pride, the vanity, the Arrogance He felt the Power as the Wings did lift Him off the Floor. He felt alive and Younger, much stronger but only for a moment. He now Understood the Power of the Angels and Demons, if Only for a moment, He still tasted the Power and felt it go thru out all of His Body, He was alive, only for a moment and Now All He has is the memory" but How did You turn off the bathroom light by Just waving Your hand?" I will Practice after everyone leaves and see if I still have this Power, Time will Tell, " What will I Do with this Gift? Is it a Gift from God or the Goddess or some Demonic force? If I can Shapeshift into this demonic Entity can I shape-shift into something Else? So far only my hands seem to change will other parts of my body change also?" I felt this Power surge thru me sort of like when the Wings grew on my Back I felt the power I could actually fly, if only for a Moment, I felt what the Angels and Demons must have felt. Yes, the power was Sensational, the Energy was great, He felt the Power, if Only for a Moment and He will have that to remind Him at what cost? He will Not Forget the Other Power, when Lightning broke His wing off, everyone heard it snap and He felt the Pain. "I do Not want to go thru that again Never Again". Now that I told you a Story You Have To ask Yourself Did This Really Happen Right Before We got here? Or Could This have Happened a Long time ago and the Old Man is Playing with our Imagination? Does the Old man Have a Lot of tattoo's? Or is this Just another Wild Dream?" The Four Camera Crew and the Fifth Lady From Amazon looked at each Other to See What Each one Thought about it. Smiling the Old Man said "Ok I will Take off My Shirt,You Will See Me Running around In My Bathing Suit sooner or Later so We Need to Get this Over Now". The Camera Crew Filmed the Old man Taking off His Shirt and revealing his Many Tattoo's all Over His Chest and Upper arms. No One in Public has Ever seen Him without a Shirt,Yes, He Was the Multi-Billionaire who Was a Motivational Speaker People Paid Thousand's of Dollars to Hear One of His Seminars. He was always so Professional, Three Piece Suit and Tie and He had Nice Gray Hair so They Were Surprised to See a Shaven Bald Headed Younger Version of all The Pictures of Him they Have Seen." End of Chapter seven

Chapter Eight:
Knight in Shining Armor
Act Eight Scene Eight

She Clips a Microphone to my Shirt and they say "anytime you are ready",the Film starts up, as He sets on the couch. "We already Talked about Your Fingerprint,You can Write a Book about these Things, but Sometimes we have to go thru these things to Experience them, and Teach us, some ways toward Enlighten-ment. So our Circular Staircase, and Maybe the Story of Me

Sprouting Demonic Wings and Shapeshifting can be Treasure Number Ten and Some People May See thirteen or Fourteen Treasure's out of the Book or Movie Some of My Secrets You May already Have Heard, but I am Telling you again so I will Add a Few Extra ok?" I Paused Took a Drink then went on " I want to share a Little more info as it Comes to Me, I Hope You Realize I am only saying what Pops up in My Mind or What I feel It tell's me to, so One Moment, I will talk about one thing, then all of a Sudden out of the Blue talk about something else, Remember this. I realize getting a lot of Different People to Come together under one Church or Religion is far fetched. I do Believe there are a lot of People out there, who for Various reasons are not happy with the Religion and Church, they were Taught. All you know is what you were taught I said it before and I will keep on saying it,If you are not happy with the Church or Religion you were Taught then you do have the Right to Go looking for another. I looked for over Twenty Years,Trying to Find God,Then I realized There has to be a Female Creator in this Process. As a Male Species, I can See Why a Lot of Males Do Not Want Woman to Have Equal Rights,They Want to Run things. If The Average Person Would Be Happy as Equal, then we would Not have a Problem, But Give Some Woman Power and It goes to Their Head. I seen Some Woman, when you Give them a Badge,a gun and authority, it goes to their Head and they are very mean,Yes They are Dealing with Bad People,Yes they Broke the Law but they are still Human beings with Feelings and Emotions.On the Other Hand, I seen some Woman Glad to Have the Power and Treat all as Equal, Again all you Know is What you were Taught,Maybe a Man at One time did Abuse You and I understand that, Sometimes we Need to Learn the Hard way and Its the Learning Process we all are Constantly going thru That is another Reason I believe Avalon Ministry Is a Good Thing,It gives a Lot of Different People from all walks of Life the Opportunity to Join together under one Roof to Meet and Talk about our Culture Differences..I believe We Should Keep God's Law of the True 7th day Saturday Sabbath, as our Day of Rest. This was a Commandment, Jesus Never Worshipped on Sunday, the 1st day of the Week,He was a Good Jewish/Hebrew who Kept the 7th day Saturday Sabbath. I also Believe in the Kosher Food Laws, The Jewish,Islam and some Christians do Not Eat Pork, Catfish, Lobster or Shrimp, These are still Called "Scavenger foods" I will Try to Teach People the Importance of this,Some Will Still want to Eat what ever they want to, but Most, Once they Realize the Bacteria and Germs, then Hopefully Refrain from eating Unclean Scavenger foods. I grew up as a Baptist.My Grandpa Raised Pigs, so I grew Up Eating Pork. Some of My Family are Still Stubborn Baptist and Still Eat Pork. I found Out there is Turkey Bacon,Turkey

Ham and Turkey Sausage, so its Better for me. I am Still Waiting on Turkey pork Chop,but Until then i will eat Lamb Chops, which are very Good. Thats enough of that for Now. So Now Another Story, Do You Remember Your First Love?" He Looks around at everyone Shaking their heads In Agreement" How about Your First Kiss?" again they all Nod their head" For Me, It was a Long time ago, Yes, I was Going thru My Puberty, a Time When Little Boy's Wake Up with a Hard On, and Go to Bed with a hard on" They All laugh and Smiling they Nod their Heads, Smiling back, I Contiue " I Was Twelve and in the Sixth grade, Back Then, I Had a Lot of Thick Red Hair and Freckles" Smiling He Rubbed His Bald Head, Everyone Laugh's as He Continued " Hardly Any Girl ever Noticed Me, Yes My Family were Rich But They Wanted Me to Go to a Public School and they Hid This from them,They Thought the Butler Who Picked Me up In the Old Station Wagon was My Dad, It was My Secret, Dad was Off In Europe somewhere making Big Million Dollar Deals.Then One day, out of the Blue, the Prettiest Girl in School, Peggy Sue, Walked over to Me, Beautiful Blonde Hair and Big Blue eyes, She Looked at Me and said, Do You want to Be My Friend? My Heart was Pounding Ninety Miles a Hour and I Got this Tremondous Erection" Everyone is Laughing, as I Hold My Hand Up, Smiling, Trying to Continue "Yes, I was Embarrassed, Hoping She would Not Look Down and Notice and Take off Running,She Didn't and I was Relieved. She Held My Hand and Said, You Will Be My Knight In Shining Armor, To Protect Me from Evil, Fire Breathing Dragons. Yes, I was Willing to Be anyone She wanted me to Be. Now I Know, What your First Love is all about, My Heart was Beating so Fast,The Excitement,The Goosebumps from Her Holding My Hand, then She Looks around to See If anyone was Watching,She Let Go of My Hand then With Both of Her Hands, She Touched My Face,Then Kissed Me. I Guess She Saw Her Daddy, Kiss Her Mom that way, It was Over in a Moment, But I can Still Taste that Sweetness of that First Kiss." I stopped For a Moment To Take a Drink then Went on " She said' Do You Want to Get on the Seesaw?" "Yes" I replied, Willing to Go anywhere or do anything she wanted to, I weighed More then She did so I could Tell I had to Take it easy, as I Went Down, I would Stretch out My Feet to Slow down the Bend, and Push back up Ever so Gently, She was Smiling, Yes, She was Happy. I Guess Every School Has their Bully and This Elementary School was No Exception, He Failed School Twice, so He was Much older and Fatter. No one Liked Him, Because If He Seen You Bringing your Lunch, He would Grab it,Eat all Your Cupcakes or Desert and Push you around. He came over to My Side of the seesaw and Said for Me to Get Off.He Put His foot to Keep The Seesaw from Moving, i looked over at her She was Way Up in the air and She was Shaking her Head No,She did Not want to Play with him. I told Him "No, Go away" With His Left hand He Grabbed a Head Full of My Red Hair,Yes It Hurt. He had Rotten Teeth and Bad Breath as He Showed me His Right hand then Got into My Face and said "Ok Punk do you want a Black Eye? A Broke Nose? or a Busted Lip?" Trembling Not Knowing what to Do I Panicked, I got Up and He sat Down Peggy Started Screaming, He Said "Its Ok, I Am Not going to Hurt you, He Pushed Up real fast then as He came Down He Moved His Legs, so He Hit with a Thud. I thought She was Going to Fly thru the Air. She Kept on Screaming as They Went Up and Down.I stood Back in Horror. I was Supposed to Be Her Knight in Shining Armor and Slay the Mean Evil Fire Breathing Dragon. She was Guinivere, the Damsel In Distress, I was Help-less.Our Small English Teacher Came out Telling the Big Bully To stop. He Took one Look at Her Small Body and Laughing Kept on. As He Came down with a Thud She Stepped on the Seesaw Holding it Down with Her Foot. With Her Left Hand, She Grabbed His Right Ear and Twisted it as Hard as She Could,In Pain, He Lashed Out with His Right Hand and She Grabbed it and Twisted It around He started Standing and I ran over to Grab the Seesaw as He Got off and Started Fighting Her I Let the Seesaw down so Peggy Could get off.She Hung on to His Ear with One Hand and Twisted His Right arm around His Back as He Turned around She Kicked Him as Hard as She Could Right Behind His Knee and He went down. Another Male Teacher who saw It all From a Distance Came Running over Took the Bully Into the principal office and he Got a Good Spanking. Back Then, If you Misbehaved then You did Get a Good Spanking. I ran over to Peggy Sue Who was Crying,thru Her tears She said " I thought You were My Knight In Shining armor? You Were Supposed to Rescue me from all the Fire Breathing Dragons, But You Did Not. You Are Not My Friend, No More. I do Not Like You, go away" I was Devastated.You are Only a Kid,No One Tells You What to Do.Knowing Now, I should Have Taken Some Martial art Classes,Which I did Later on. Maybe I could Have done Something different Everyone Knows, Woulda, Shoulda, Coulda, Now I Play this Scenero back in My Mind,When He Grabbed My Hair with His Left hand, that Left His Left Side Vulnerable.If You Raise Your Left arm Up then Feel the Tender spot Under your arm" I Paused took a Drink and Could see Everyone raising their Left arm to see What I was Talking about and they, Shaking their Heads in agreement now Understanding that is a Vulnerable spot, I continue." With My Left Elbow, I could Hit Him as Hard as i Could like this" Showing Everyone a Basic Karate Blow Using My Left elbow Hitting His Imaginary Chest." Now He Would Definitely Let Go of My Hair. In Pain His Right Hand Would Still aim for My Face. So Remember the Movie Karate Kid" I Pause Look at everyone they Shake their

Head, I take another drink then go on "Wax on, wax off" as I Sway My Right arm up to Block His oncoming Blow. Now I Grab His Right arm with Both of My Hands and Do the same thing the Small Teacher Did. Yes She was Small But She Did Take some Self Defense Classes and It Paid off when the Big Fire Breathing Dragon Tried to Fight Her.of Course, I was Humiliated, Enbarrassed,A Small Woman Fought this Mean Bully and Made a Fool out of Me. It was Not Her Fault. I am Glad She came along, I Needed to Learn a Lesson. My First Love, My First Kiss was over, Peggy Sue Found another Boy friend. I often Thought about If I did Take some Self Defense Classes, Yes, My Dad asked Me was I ready for that and I told Him No, What would it Be like if I did Take the Karate Classes and beat Up the Bully? I could have Eventually Marry Peggy Sue and Our Children would be Different,Yes Different names, Different Finger-prints,Different Facial Qualities.I Love My Children and Grand Children. These Things Happen for a Reason. I needed to Fall in love,Have My Heart Broken, 30 Minutes later and Now Get to Experience these things" I Pause for a Moment Showing my Coffee Cup is Empty,the Maids Brought in some donuts, so we take a Short Break, Their Camera is off but the Ghost Camera Is still Rolling, Showing all the Behind the Scene activity. The Camera goes to The Boxing arena again showing the Same Beautiful girl in the Bikini and showing the same Big Sign saying Ten Minutes Later This Time. Everyone is amused. Back to work, He sets down in His Oak Rocking Chair this time, He loves this old antique chair, The Girls are ready they Motion Him to Start when Ever You Are ready, He Takes a drink of Coffee and sets it on the Coffee Table as He looks in the Camera He resumes His Dialogue. "Where were we? Yes, I remember We are having so many Different Wars and Continuous Fighting." The Camera Crew and Your Imagination can Imagine scenes from a Different Location Different People, different Costumes, etc. " Say for example you have two People in the army both are wearing the same Green Uniform, one is a Private and the Other is a General, How do you tell the difference between the two? They are both wearing the same shirt,Same Pants, Same boots and same Hats? One is a Private and the Other is a General, how do you tell the Difference? We all Know they have these little Medals on the Private, has a one bar Chevron and the General has a Chrome star, this is how you Know Which Person to Salute and Show respect to." We Stop and take another Break this time for Lunch Their camera Stops But the Ghost Camera Keeps Going, she Does Not Need to Take a break, She does not eat or drink or go to the Bathroom like we do. She is a Spirit/Soul that thrives off of Energy. Just like a Vampire drinks Blood to Survive She is one of the original VamPowers who Thrive off your Power or Energy, Yes she can go into Human form into another physical mortal flesh and blood human to temporary Experience, feed, drink,and absorb your energy, sometimes thru the sexual act during intercourse drain-ing the orgasm from Her Victims, the Life line of all creation. they lay their smiling,drained and all energy gone not realizing were all the Energy went to. They have to go to sleep to Re-charge themselves then go thru the process over and over not knowing what is going on.The Blind Sheep, who is the Predator?" we stop for Lunch again if the Film crew wants to keep recording thats cool everyone relaxed enjoying a great meal. End of Chapter Eight

Chapter Nine:
Ten Cow Woman
Act Nine   Scene Nine:

The crew are once again ready we go back into the large living room the old man goes to his bar and mixes a drink, He tells all the crew anytime they want a drink to help themself,He motions for His butler to come over and play bartender, a job He loves to do, smiling, He gladly steps forward   Pause Note: To Keep this from being a boring Movie or a Boring Book you can Imagine as the Old man Is Talking maybe He is Wearing different Costumes, Remember He is Very Rich and Crazy, so He Likes to Dress Up or Down according to His Latest feelings and Emotions. Maybe disquised as someone or Something different to Keep the Excitement going, The Old Man Talks:" Would the World Be a Better Place if we all Would Learn a Little about other Religions, then Decide what is Right For Us. What May Be Right For you, May Not Be Right For Me,My Favorite Color is Red, so everyone who Likes Red Can Join My Church,Your Favorite Color Maybe Blue,Sorry You are not Invited, You have to go down the Street and Start your own Blue Church,Some of the Doctrines are that Simple. Then you have a Hundred Shades of Red ,so Now You Have More Denominations and More "Versions" of The Holy Bible and More Different Churchs on each Corner, Ok so now lets Tell another story, a long Time ago there was a Tribe of People, there was No Such thing as Money, they Had Animals and other things as Value to Trade, so when the Chief decided His Son was Ready to Become a Man and Get Married, He thought He was Old Enough and was Taught well to Handle His Own Life, so He Gave Him Ten Cows out of His Herd. Now the Value is, it starts with the Lowest which is Chickens, then Pigs, Sheep and Cows as the Highest, so You Figure so Many Chickens will Buy a Pig and So Many Sheep would be Equal to a Cow so they Traded to Survive. One of the Cows was actually a Male Bull, Who Has the Power to Get all the

Cows Pregnant at different times to have Baby Calves and let the Flock grow. Now When a Woman Reaches the age to Be Married, She is Put Inside a Circle, so All The Eligible Man can see Her as She Turns, each Man Has the Power to Bid On Her and the Highest Price is the Winner, She Does Have The Option of Looking at the Highest Bidder and Turn away, If She so Chooses and the Next Bidder gets the Chance, Only When She Reaches out to Him and Accepts the Bid then They Both Become Married, Kind of Like a Dowry. The Son of the Chief Was In Love with this Young Woman and they Both New a Day Would Come when She would Have to Be Bid Upon. When All the Woman Went down to The River to wash the clothes, they Would Brag about What their Husbands gave for Them, One Would say, My Husband gave Two Pigs and Three Chickens for Me, Another Laughing would say That is Nothing My Husband gave Two Cows and One Sheep For Me, The Stories went on and On. When Her Day Came, Only The Eligible Man formed the Circle and The Chief said Ok, we Will Start the Bidding. Before anyone Else Had the Chance to Stand up the Son of the Chief Stood Up and Said "I Will Give all ten Of My Cows for Her". The Chief was Surprised and So was Everyone else, No One Has Ever Gave That Many Cows for One Woman, It was Unheard of. Even the Woman Blushed and Looked at Him Smiling, She Put out Her Hands to Accept and Everyone Cheered. Yes, they Were Married. All The Other Man said we all Knew She was For you and You could Have Gotten Her for a Lot less. No One Else would Bid against You. He Turned and Looked at His Future wife and Said. I Know, I Just Wanted Her and Everyone Else to Know that I Love Her So Much I was Willing to Give Everything for Her. The Story of the Ten Cow Woman spread for Thousands of Years, Yes He Slowly Built Up His Worth again and People Still Talk about How Love can Solve all Problems. Sometimes You Have to Be Willing to Give Everything, for What You Want, and Let the World Know That, Some People Learn this Secret or is it a Elusive Treasure? They Apply it to their Own Lives, Its Up to You, So now it would be easy to say, all we need is Love, that will solve all our problems but Everything has to have a Opposite, this is another Hidden Elusive Treasure, you see Everything has a Opposite, the First Wisdom we learn is called Duality, the Symbol of Duality is a Coin showing their are Two sides, a head and a Tail,Just like our Emotions have two sides Love and hate, so you see it would be impossible to do a way with Hate. Actually the World would be Pretty Boring if everyone did Love everyone, after a While. Its like a Male and a Female, They too were created Different, Up and down are the Opposite Left and Right, Forward and Backwarg good and Evil. So Who Created Lucifer? We will talk about Him and/or Her again in another Chapter but If Our God did

Create everything then did Our Male God Create Evil? If we accept the Idea that God does have a Wife and they Together thru Perfect Love Perfect Trust, Created Everything then the Opposite was created which was Evil. Do you, as a Creator Destroy this Evil you created? What if you tried again would the Opposite be Born? I Teach our Male God, Yahweh and His Wife, The Shekhinah, Did Create a Child, He ws Named Lucifer, the First born Son(Sun) and also a First born Daughter called Auriel You call Her Mother Earth,Then there were many other Arch angels Created, we Know about Raphael, Michael and Gabrael, so in Wicca Auriel is Mother Earth,Her Direction is North Her Color is Green. Raphael is the Air spirit Arch angel who Rules over East,and is the color White, then Michael is the South, Fire Spirit and is the color Red and Gabrael, She is the West Water Spirit and the color Blue Thats It for the day,maybe Tomorrow another secret Now Relax Jump in the Pool or Ocean eat and Go over the Film Footage." stop end of Chapter

Chapter Ten:
Grasshopper Story
Act Ten Scene Ten
New Day

The Old man is Talking:"The Next Elusive Treasure is, Your Mortal,Flesh and Blood Human Body Will Die,You can Pay the Funeral Home a Lot of Money for a Fancy Casket, Embalming Fluid and a Concrete Vault, You are Only making the Funeral home Rich and Prolonging the Inevitable They Are Laughing at you all the Way to the Bank,Your Spirit/Soul Left your Body and is Judged, Are You going to Tell God and the Goddess that You were saved By Grace? It Does Not Work that way. I do Believe That Jesus Christ Is On the Right Hand side of God and Will Speak on Your Behalf,So Could the Goddess be on the Left side of God? What did People Believe in Before Jesus was Born? There was No Jesus on the Right hand side of God Intercedding on Your Behalf, Yes there was a Judgement day, Yes God and The Goddess will Judge you, each Life, Lucifer was the First born Son But He was Cast out of Heaven so Now, As Christians our Faith teaches that Jesus Will Help at Judgement day.Yes I was Born a Christian I was Saved and Baptized and Believe Jesus Christ is the Son of God, But so Is Lucifer,.I still accept the Teachings of Jesus Christ and Want to Learn the Teachings of Mohammed, Buddah and The Hindu teachings, Is that so Bad? Ok Now another story or a Treasure, I remember when I was a Kid I found this Grasshopper and I put it in a Old mayonaise Jar,I punched holes in the lid and Put some grass for it to eat then watched it .Several Times the grasshopper Tried to Jump up but Hit His Head and finally Quit trying..When I went to bed I could hear the grass-hopper jumping up, Hitting his head finally He Gave up. The next morning I felt sorry for the grasshopper so i went outside ,took the lid off then said jump out you are now free, a Few Hours went by and I went into lunch, after i came back I seen the grasshopper still Inside. He Got Tired of Trying and Just gave up. What is the Difference between a Rich person and a Poor Person? The Rich Person Never gives up, He Keeps on Trying over and over, Even If He looses Everything,Like I did, they Have the Knowledge that sooner or Later they will Finally Achieve what they want. Which One are you?" this time we are out side.We have a Swimming pool with a Man made waterfall pumping water out of the Pool and Circulating back in and adding the Chlorine as needed. This is Our little Picture of the garden Of Eden,Its a Nice day so we decided to film outside. Everything is set Up .Microphone on my shirt collar ready to go: " I always ask a Lot of Questions That is How You find out the Answer even when I was a Kid, I always wanted to Know things,Dad Bought me the latest Encyclopedia and Computers and Private Tutors to Teach Me all the Things, a Rich Child Should Know. One of the Big Questions we already asked was, Does God have a Fingerprint? We were Created in the Image of A God so it would make sense that if He wanted to identify us by Giving us a Unique Different Fingerprint, then He would Have one Also. Does the Goddess,or the Female side of a God, Does She, have a Fingerprint? Does the Sons and Daughters, we call Angels and Demons, Have a Fingerprint? So Now If, When we Die from our Mortal, Flesh and Blood Human Body and we are Judged ,Do we Carry this same fingerprint with us from one Re-incarnation to another? We Know we have Lived many Past Lives, I have gone into Self Hypnosis and Recall some of my Previous Lives. I was never a King or President or If I was, I do Not remember, One Past life I Have had several dreams about, so they folt real ,Did I leave my Fingerprint in My Dream? We know back in the time, the Black plague was going on and a Lot of Good People did Die, all My Family, my Wife and Children, all did die from the Black Plague, Why was I spared? I Believed I was spared Because, during that time, I studied The Magical arts, some were good magic and others were what was called dark magic, I was a Real Vampire, which means I did not drink blood but absorb the Energy, the Power from my Victims, You would Now call Us Physic Vampires ,for you see a Real Vampire Never drinks Blood, He or She is Not afraid of the Cross or the Sun, that is all Superstition, to fool the common People. We can Touch you and Pull your Energy from You. We can use Our 5 senses and Merely Look at you, and My Eyes will Touch you and I can draw your Power from you. If I

Hear your voice, say even on a Telephone, all the way across to Europe, i can Touch you, thru my Hearing. After all My Family died from the Black Plague, I found solace in the Bottle of Rum, to satisfy the Demons inside of me, only to wake up the Next day, hungry and wanting to feed, from a new victim and back to the Bottle of rum, to quiet the Demons, if only for a While. The People who ran the Ships were Having a hard time getting sailors to Run their ships and the Pirate trade were no different, one Night a Stranger bought me several rounds of Rum, and as I passed out, they Loaded me on their Ship ,the Next morning, I woke with a Hang-over for away from land. I had a Choice, Jump over board and feed the sharks or work the Boat. Not Much of a Choice, but I wanted to live. Then One day,They got into a fight with another ship, and a Man come running at me with a sword,I had to defend my self or die,I killed him,stole what he had on him, including His Nice Sword and tossed his Body over board to the Sharks, he would have done the same for me,Killing got easier,at the Time I knew Killing was wrong, I grew up as a Christian, back then and I knew sooner or later I will Have to make my Peace with my God.. The Ship eventually was hit, and we all started sinking, every man for him self, the captain and a Few of His right hand man, grabbed the only few lifeboats, i found a Door that was tore off because of the cannon explosion and grabbed it, Hoping it would float,It did. I fell asleep on the board and woke up the next morning to a Bright sunny day, no one in Sight, If anyone did Survive, they were long gone. I drifted for three days and Three Nights delirous, laughing that I am Surrounded by all this food and i am starving, surrounded by all this water and I was Dying of thirst. I tried drinking the salt water, it only made me sick, finally out of desperation I called on this God and Goddess to forgive me. I know I had no right to ask, but I accepted My Fate and to weak to stay on I rolled off the board. A Beautiful, Naked, Blonde woman with blue eyes, swam Up behind Me and rescued Me, Even in my Weakness I was Aroused, she was Beautiful, I felt this Must be Heaven, I did Not Deserve this, But I am Not Complaining, Finally My feet touched sandy Bottom and I walked a Shore, I turned to Get the Woman who Helped me, she waved and swam off, She was a Mermaid, half woman, Half fish. I will Never forget the dreams over and over. It seemed so real. I made a Vow to change my ways and I became a Preacher, trying to Teach others the Amazing Power of Our Creator God and Goddess. Another past life I was a Outlaw, I was a Very Bad person, who Killed and stole from People, this was During the 1800's. I fell in Love with this Beautiful red head, Who Happened to be married to the Town Sheriff. One Night in a Drunken Brawl, He Shot Me in the Back, to coward to face me, as I laid dying, she came up to Me and Whispered In My Ear, that She was Pregnant with My Child.My Last words were to Tell Him It is His, So he want Hurt You. I made My Peace with My God and I was Judged I was Born Inside the Womb of the Red head, I was in Love with, Yes Now I became Her Red Headed Daughter and She Knew who I was in a Previous Life. I spent My Whole Life Taking care of the Woman who in One Life was My Lover and another Life was My Mother, Stranger Things have Happened I guess. The Sheriff was Shot a Short time Later By another drunk Who Out drew Him. Wait you ask what is the Secret Here? Just another Story or What? Some May See another Secret, Maybe they too Have had Past Life Regression, There Has to Be Something to this Reincarnation. It makes sense. Could the Secret Be if You are Going into a Self Hypnosis Mode and Telling Your Mind to Go Back in time, to Maybe a Past Life or Maybe you are Having a Recurring dream You Need the Key To Open this Door.A song says sometimes we live our lives in chains not knowing we have the Key. Maybe Some Other People Can Help you." We stop again for lunch then start again in the next Chapter. ten

Chapter Eleven:
Wheel Barrel Blindfold Story
Act Eleven Scene Eleven:

The old man is ready again microphone in place "The Next Doctrinal Question, is Jesus Christ The Messiah(Ha Mashiach)? According to Luke's "Version" you are Reading then NO, He Can Not Be. Why Would God Pick Joseph,Knowing He was from the Right Bloodline of the Tribe of Judah,With the Right Dna to Bring Forth the True Messiah(Ha Mashiach) then Not Use Him? This is Why Most Jewish and Islam Believe that Jesus was a Good Teacher, But He was Not the Messiah. If You Accept Luke's Version then Joseph was Not Legally Married to the Virgin Mary,The Angel told Joseph to Not Lay with her,If They Did Not Have Sex then the Marriage was Not Legal.Did God Marry the Virgin Mary? No, Luke said The Spirit of God Went Into the Virgin Mary "AND" the Holy Spirit Went into the virgin Mary. So Why would Two Entities Go into the Virgin Mary? Most Christian Church's were Taught, You Have a Male God, A Male Son of God and a Male Holy Spirit and That is Your 3 Male Trinity, It takes Three of Something to Make a Trinity, Right? So who is the Holy Spirit? Can God be two or three separate Entities? Did He go into the Virgin Mary? Hope not, Did God Break His Own laws of Deuteronomy22? What do you call a Child Born out of Wedlock? That is What other Religions Think of Our Christ. What else can they Think? All they Know is What they Were Taught, Is Luke

Right? Or Is Luke Only writing down what People Tell Him their "Version" of What they Think actually Did Happen? Stop right now and read that. Now the Truth,What really did Happen Luke's Version was Wriiten around 50ad almost twenty Years after Christ was Killed, a lot of Time has Elapsed and the Stories handed down.What if the Spirit of God Actually Did Go into Joseph? Knowing He had the Right Bloodline from the Tribe of Judah and the Right Dna to Bring forth the True Messiah(Ha Mashiach) and The Goddess, the Wife of God, Did Go into the Virgin Mary. God Had Sex with His Wife in the Spiritual World, Joseph Had Sex with His Wife in the Physical World There was No Laws Broken, The Marriage was Legal,The Child Born was the Son of a Carpenter, With the Right Bloodline from the Tribe of Judah to Bring forth the True Messiah(Ha Mashiach) and also More Important, the Son of God You Have a Choice, Accept Luke's Version and Believe that Our Jesus Can Not Be the Messiah according to His "Version" are Accept Maybe all Luke Knows Is What He was Taught, also Remember Who would Benefit by this? The same Angel that Told Eve it was ok to Eat the Forbidden apple, This Is Lucifer's World, like it or Not,He is the Ruler,Yes Lucifer is the Real true First born Son of our God,You Have a Choice" Pause . "Now another Story or a Treasure, a Guy said He Could Walk a Tight Rope Blindfolded across Niagra Falls, Pushing a Wheel Barrel. Of Course this Feat has Never Been Done, so No one Believed Him, His Preacher Told Him it was Very Dangerous and He would Be Killed, He Looked the Preacher in the Eye and Said You Told Me If I Believed in the Power of a Mustard Seed, I Could Move a Mountain, Well I Do Not Want to Move a Mountain, I Believe I can do this. I want You To Be There, Yes, Pray For Me and Be there on the Other side, When I Get across, The Preacher agreed. The Man Pushed the Wheel Barrel, Blindfolded, and Made it to The Other side, Everyone was Cheering as He Took The Blindfold Off and The Preacher came up to Shake His Hand and Hug Him, the Man said "Now Preacher Do You Believe? Yes" The Preacher Replied "I Do Believe, I Seen It with My On Eyes, No" The Man said "Do You Really Believe?" "Yes" The Preacher said again" I Saw it, If You Truly Believe,Then Get Into the Wheel Barrel and We Will Both Go Back Across." Its One Thing to Believe in something, the Secret Number Seven is To Be able to Move a Mountain, with Just the Faith of a Mustard seed. Now There are People Out there who are Atheist. I want to share with you a True story that is very Important. A Woman ate some pork that was not cooked all the way thru, This Bacteria went thru her arteries and veins and some wound up in her Brain ,the Bacteria started growing in Her brain and became a Tumor, the size of a Big Golf ball,She went to the doctor because she was having fainting spells, were she would black out, they did some test and scans and found the tumor in Her brain. They had to shave Her hair off, Cut a Big hole in Her skull. Remove the Tumor then she had to go thru Chemo-theraphy, because of the Chance of it being Cancerous. This woman had to go thru all of this ordeal, all because she went to a Fast food Resturant and ate Pork. Why Do they call it a Fast food Resturant? Because they fix the food, fast. That is Enough on that Matter. Now another Elusive Treasure for those reading every word. I want to Talk about One of my Dreams I had, It was Kind of Like the Movie, Back to the Future, were a Silver Delorean takes off in the air and time travels into the Future or past. there were several H.G. wells Movies about time machines, so its cool and maybe that was in My Subconscious but in my Dream, I was asleep.The alarm clock woke me up and I took a Shower, shaved, ate breakfast, started to drive to Work, like I usually do.I pushed the garage door opener, to see It was raining and Thundering and I was Driving My Old Red Volkswagen bug, i had 30 Years ago. I backed out of the Drive-way and started down the street, The Bug took off in the air and I time traveled in the Past. I wound up in the desert, Right before Jesus Was Crucified. I spent six Years there, I could Not Figure How to get back, I Married a Widow woman who already Had two Boys and we had another son and another daughter. Could I have Lived during this Past Lifetime? Was My Fingerprint the same Fingerprint I have today? Then One Night I went to Sleep,as Usual. I woke Up the next Morning to the Sound of the Alarm clock waking me Up, Startled I jumped out of Bed Looked at my watch and the day and realized during this 8 Hours of Sleep I lived six Years of My Life, I could tell You In great Detail all the Little things I done each day ,My Childrens name, the Sheep I was taking care of, My Wife of Six years going thru the Birth of each baby and Not Having a Hospital to take her to and seeing My baby Boy and Baby Girl being born and watching them crawl on the floor and learning how to walk. How Can I remember Six Years in one 8 hour Night? in this other World, Time does not mean anything, a day is as a Thousand years, i remember reading that somewhere In the BIble so the Dinosours could be Living for millions of years and that would be Just like a Month or Two, Did these Cave man have fingerprints also? Are we the Only Civilization that has a Fingerprint? When I woke Up and I realized it was Only Eight Hours gone by and I knew I had to go to work so I took my Shower, ate my breakfast and pushed open the garage door Opener to find it was Thundering and Raining. I hopped in My Red Bug and backed out of the Driveway and Paused. Do I want to Put this in Forward and Take a Chance on Going back in time? It was Pouring down rain I put it in Gear and drove back into the Garage and Closed the Garage door Opener. I called in Sick and went back to bed. I had some sick time built up, and I did not want to take a Chance going into the Past and Spending six Years, Yes It was Fun, Learning a New Language Trying to Learn a New Custom, marrying a Beautiful Woman and Having Two Beautiful Children, could that be Me from a Past Life? What Happened? Did i get Killed? How could I have Lived Six years In One 8 Hour Period? I Thought about writing a Book about my Ordeal but Realized there are so many Other Books about people who have Time traveled in the Past or In the Future and their World was a Lot More Exciting, so probably no one would read it they would Think I just Imagined it and had a Dream from My Subconscious Imagination. " So Now Were is the Secret? Is this Just another Story from a Crazy Old man? Maybe too Much Beer? were is the Elusive Treasure? Or Too Many Crazy Movie's? You Decide Ok?" We stop to take a break yes people need to go to the bathroom and take a break

Chapter Twelve:
The Two Kingdom Fight
Act Twelve scene Twelve:

The Old Man is Talking:" If you have read this Much of this Book and Have read any other of My Books you will see, I say the same thing over and over, in various Chapters and Books,Why? How do you Remember something? Only Thru Repetitions right?. They are ready, the Microphone is attached to my shirt on with the show: "First I want to Talk a little about Paul, Most of His Writings were around 60-70 ad which was thirty Years after The Death of Christ and remember The Ruler of this World is the First Born Son of our God and Goddess and that is Lucifer,Is He a Angel or Demon? Remember long before Christianity, Jewish, Islam, New Testament,Old Testament and even Moses was Born, we know that the Egyptian Pharoah's daughter rescued the Baby Moses, what did they believe in? They worshipped a Male God Osiris and a Female Goddess, Isis as Equal, Why? Equality? were they the only Culture? No many many more Cultures and Civilizations worshipped a Male God and a Female Goddess as Equal,Then What Happened? Why did we take the Female out of Religions? Did we, as Males not want the Female to have this Equality? Remember when Jesus was alive, the Romans worshipped a Male God they called Jupiter and a Female Goddess they called Juno, You can still go to Rome and see the Remains of the Various temples and even Greeks had a Male God they called Zeus and a Equal Goddess they called Hera, Even today, you can still go to Egypt,Greece or Rome and still see the Remnants, so what gives you the Right to remove the Female Goddess out of any and Every Religion? According To Moses when Lucifer was talking to Eve, He was a very handsome Angel, then God Turned Him into a Snake,Right? When Paul was on the Road to Damascus a Bright Light Blinded Him for Three Days and This Bright Light Told Him its ok to Eat Scavenger foods and Do what ever you want to, you are No Longer under the Law. So Do You Worship God or Paul? Now a Story Most People Have heard Different Version's of this Story My Version is there was Two Kingdoms and They Both had a Thousand man Army,this was a Long time ago. One King thought, If We Could Sneak Up on this Other Kingdom and Surprise them,Then We could Kill all their Man,Take their Woman and Livestock and have all this for them selves,Yes Greed was the Secret. The Devious King Figured If He Took all His Man and Surrounded the Other Kingdom, then attack from all Different Directions, all at Once, then They Could Not Run away,The Element of Surprise and a Early Morning Attack while they were Just Getting Up, Would Be the Ultimate Surprise.So The Bad King Decided He and Two Hundred and Fifty of His Soldiers would attack from the North. Now He Divided Two Hundred and Fifty of His Man to Go to the West, Two Hundred and Fifty to go to The East and the Last Two Hundred and Fifty to go all the way Around to the South. He Would Give Them Three Days to March at Night and Sleep during the day, In total Secrecy on the Morning of the Third day they would all attack at Sunrise. Sometimes Strategically This would Work. While the King and His 250 men were waiting they decided to Have a Party and Get Drunk,Who Knows Some will Die. What they did Not Know was there were Spies in the Land that went and told the other King of Their Plans. What do you do? Wait for the Third day and Let Them attack? No The Good King got White Tunic Shirts made for all thousand of His Men and Painted Bright Red Cross on the Front and Back so Everyone could see They Were the Good Guys. Kill Anyone Not Wearing a White Tunic with a Bright Red Cross. That Night While the King and His 250 Drunk Men were Sleeping they Attacked and Killed all of them Including the King, They Chopped His Head Off and Stuck it on a Long Pole, so Everyone could see Their King was Dead. The Other 250 From the East were doing the same thing they Knew tomorrow they may die, so they had a Party and all Got drunk waiting on the South to Get There and Be Ready, So The Good King Attacked them By Surprise again Who wins? 250 Men or Thousand? Once You see, They Surprised you and You see Your Dead King's Head On a Pole. So anyway to make a Long Story Short The Good King Did win. Now What is the Secret? "United We Stand, Divided we Fall" Everyone Has Heard that, so Now There is Power in Numbers" We pause because its Lunch time, The Pretty Girl in the Boxing arena in the Bikini Shows the big sign One Hour Later."Realize there are Million, Billion, Trillion different People all

On their Own Path, all doing what they need to do to Experience what they need to do during this lifetime and each person having to do what they need to do to Experience all the Different things they want to do and then something Happens. Some Drunk runs a red Light and crashes in your car and accidently Kills you. Did you get to Experience all the Things you wanted to Do during this lifetime? No, Why? Some Drunk ran a red Light and Killed Me. So Now Your Physical Flesh and blood Body is dead and your Spirit/Soul is Judged its Not Your Fault you still got a Lot of Things you wanted to do but Life is a Bitch then you die, so Now what Happens? Do You Have to Start all Over go into a Womb and Spend 9 Months Upside down surrounded by Water, then come out Kicking and Screaming and learn How to Talk, walk and go thru learning the ABC of Life. Can you Just go to The School and say give me My High School Diploma? No, You Have to Go thru your 12 years maybe you can Skip a Year or Better Off You Maybe allowed to Attach your self to another Flesh and Blood Human who is trying to do Similar things to What you were doing. This is what we call a Split Personality, a Spirit/Soul attaches to another Spirit/Soul,Kind of like a jeckyl and hyde but some-times one is Not Good and One is Not Evil, so can we Have a Person with a Split Personality? Can We have a Person With Multiple Personality? Can these be Entities that did Not get the chance to Experience all the things they wanted to Experience and their particular life was Shortened due to a Freak Accident? Can there really be Freak Accidents? Is everything in Life Pre-ordained? Can that guy who was Drunk run the Red light Because that is what He Needed to Experience? maybe He Needed to Experience Going to Jail, Going to Court, being Sued and go thru the Humiliation of Knowing your Drunken attitude Killed a Family and Changed their Life and Now Its Changing your Life. How Many People are Now affected because of One simple Ordeal? At one Point in My Life I was way up on top soaring with the Eagles and I Had a Bad car Accident that Knocked me all the way to the Bottom ,Yes I had to Get Knocked down to the Bottom,I needed to Lose Everything to wake me Up and realize What I did have. I hope No one has to go thru that, but I realize that sometimes we need to Go thru these Obstacles and failures, what was it that God said He Built You Mountains so You would Learn How to Climb?. I had to Get Everything Taken away from Me to realize What I did have, Its a Long way from the Bottom back to were you were at. We are not satisfied to stay at one step on this spiral staircase. We can Look up and Imagine why We Have two arms,One is to raise it Up and Hope someone on a Higher step will see my arm and teach me what We need to know, to Move up that One step. My Other arm is reaching down to someone below me, to Hopefully teach them how to Move up one step Higher. We are Not Looking up,Our Faith has my one arm holding up but We are looking down at my fellow Brother and sister, Trying to Teach them what they need, so they can grab my out reached hand and pull them self Up. That is What this book is, We are Reaching out to My Fellow Brothers and Sisters. You do Not see it But My Hand is Out there Ready for you to wake up and Realize some of the Things We are saying Maybe are True. Are you ready to Grab my Hand and Pull Your self up one step Higher? If So I am Looking at you and You will Have Only one hand sticking up but your other hand is reaching out to someone else below you to Help pull them up to at least were you were Thats whats its all about Its called the Brotherhood. Its good for our Brothers and our sisters both.I do want to apologize for Repeating my self over and over. I want you the Reader to get your Money worth only thru repeating hopefully you will say Im crazy or understand and absorb some of these truths, the big Question is not wether I'm right or I'm wrong, The Question you have to ask your self is what if I am Right? If so what part of what i am saying is right and What part of what I am saying is wrong? Who gets to decide? I use the same scenero in a dream I had probably right after I seen the Movie Titanic its the same way the lifeboat is there, me in the water with one hand reaching out to the guy in the lifeboat, me looking the other way reaching out to someone else in the water.I thought it would make a cool back tattoo or great painting, the point is, you have a choice,reach out with both hands and save your self and be happy or really care about your fellow neighbor and reach out to help them out.maybe this is why God gave you two hands? what if you were that person way out in the water and you saw a person who could reach out and help you but chose not to? their pride and self worth they cared only for themselves save me once I get safely in the boat then maybe reach out to help someone else? we are all here for different reasons Why are you here? hopefully to make the World a better place " another break another day we stop all are tired.

Chapter Thirteen:
Ten Year Re-union
Act Thirteen   Scene Thirteen

New Day New act new Scene New Clothes New glass of Dr.pepper Cold Drink in hand relaxing on my sofa." The next Elusive Treasure and/or story was about two Normal High school Kids who Came from about the Same Type Family, after they Graduated One Got Married, had Children and Got a Typical Job,The Other Became very Wealthy, they had a Ten Year re-union. They Talked about all the Wild crazy Things they done, then the One Asked

What Happened, How Come you are so Rich and I am Just Getting by? The Rich Friend said Come over tomorrow to My House, He Gave Him His Address and We Will Go Swimming and I will Tell You The Secret. Excited He went Home and Told His Wife and Kids so The Next day He was Amazed to See the Address was One of the Biggest Ocean Front Properties In the Town. He Pulled Up in the Circular Drive was Greeted By the Guard who Escorted Hmi to the Front door, There the Butler Escorted Him to The Main Living room and Said "He will Be Down to see you in a Moment".The Rich Friend Came down the Stairs wearing a Bathing suit and Towel,"Ready To Go". He Looked at His Friend and Said "I thought I Told You We were Going Swimming?" " Yes", The Poor Friend Replied," I forgot all about that, I wanted To Know Your Secret Just Tell Me", The Rich Friend Replied" It Does Not Work Like That, We Have to Go Swimming First", He Call's His Butler to Bring a Extra Bathing Suit and Spare Towel, He Goes In the Guest Bathroom and Changes.They Walk around, Him Showing Everything and they Go Outside to the Ocean, the Rich Friend grabs a Life saver jacket out of the Pile and says" Lets go Swimming", The Poor Friend Looks at the Pile and Thinks He is a Good Swimmer and He Does Not Need a Life Jacket, so They Jump in and swim around, the Poor Friend said" I Thought You Were going to Tell Me your Secret" the Rich friend swam way out in the water and said "Come out here I do Not want anyone to Hear", The Water was Way over His Head But he was a Good Swimmer. "first", The Rich Friend said. "You Have to Listen to What Others say. I Told You We were Going swimming, You were Not Prepared, So You Failed Lesson One" " Ok" The Poor Friend said " I am Sorry But Now What?".The Rich Friend went on "Second Lesson I grabbed a Life saver jacket, You Did Not, Again You Do Not Come Prepared, Now the Water is Over your Head and You can Not Stay out here very Long, You Have Eyes But You Do Not See, You Have Ears But Do Not Hear" " Ok" He said " I will Learn, Please Tell Me the Secret". Then The Rich Friend Pushed Him Under water and Held Him There a Few Moments,Coming Up for air gasping saying "What are you Trying to Do? Drown Me?" The Rich Friend Replied "at that Moment, You were Under water What did You Want More than Anything More Than all The Money,Mansions, Fancy Cars Etc.?" " I wanted to Breath" , "Yes" He Replied "When You Want to Succeed, as Much as You want to Breath, then and Only Then will You Succeed" " I Found By Talking to People What they Wanted and Needed, Everything In Business is all about Supply and Demand. If Someone Demands Something then Someone else Will Supply that Need, Its Simple.You Can Have the Best Donut Shop in the World But If there are already Five Donut Shops in the area, Then You May Not Succeed. People Will Not

Drive 20 Miles to Get Your Donut, so It has to Be for a Local area, Its all about Location and Supply and Demand, Be Prepared Look the Person in the Eye, That is Something You Rarely ever do Why?" " I don't Know I guess i am Shy You Know Me, I always Have Been That way". "Yes That is Part of Your Down-fall, My Grandpa Gave Me some Good Advice a Long Time ago, Look the Person in the Eye, Tell Them What you will Do,Give a Firm Handshake and Keep Your Promise, a Man Is Only as Good as His Word. That is the Secret" Now Listen to another Story there maybe a Secret there also They Got back to Shore and layed out on the Beach enjoying each others Company and the Warth of the Sun.". I remember about Nine Years ago after we Graduated I was a Wild and Crazy Person I had long hair and a Beard plus all the Bad ass Tattoos to show my Rebellion. The Problem was Society Judges you by what you Look Like. It was hard for me to find a Decent Job, One day out of frustration I went into the Bathroom, Looked in the Mirror and I did Not Like what I seen, I shaved My beard off and cut some of my Hair,when I walked out of that Bathroom My Dog started barking at me, He Did Not Recognize me Even My Little Kids when I reached down to Pick them Up they looked at me and started crying i had to Hold them and assure them its still the same Me Inside it took a Little while to get used to the New me and even Doubting Thomas who Knew the Real Jesus Christ Did Not Recognize Him we all Know the Story so Jesus had to Flee the Town. Was Jesus actually Married? Yes Mary of Magdalene was His Wife. Did He actually Have Children? Yes Two Boys and One Girl did they all Have Fingerprints? Yes Are their Dna still out there? Yes The Children Grand children all the way down the Blood line of Jesus Christ is still out there. The Movie called the Da Vinci Code Talks a Lot of this Were did they get these Ideas from? They searched for the Truth, There are Spirit Entities out there today just like there was Spirit Entities back then. We all have our Guardian Angel watching over Us and sometimes we Want to Ignore what they arc trying to Teach us so some-times we Need to Go Back into the Womb, Learn a New Language, Learn a New Custom and Learn a New Culture so Can you Do all the Things you want to Experience in one Lifetime? Yes One of My Secret's Is The Fact the Real Jesus Christ Did Teach Re-Incarnation There is No Pearly gates,No Streets of Gold and No Mansions You are In Your Heaven/Hell Right Now You are Not saved by Grace But are Accountable this is were Avalon The Church ministry will Fit in once you Understand there is a Female Side of God and we all have One Religion inside of Us Yes we can still be Different,Speak a Different Language and Culture and Customs. You Have to Decide All You know is what you were Taught. Your Sunconscious will Only Accept What you tell it to Believe in, You Be the Judge At

Least think about What We are saying I am either right or wrong. What part of what We are saying is Right? What Part of what We are saying is Wrong? Who gets to Decide if We are Right? Who gets to Decide If We are Wrong?" Now My Friend I do Have to Go back to Work,It was Great Seeing you again Maybe we Can Get Together Hope You Think about My Secret I will Help You Get Established You Have to Decide What you want to Do,Just Imagine If You Had all the Money in the World What would you do? Sure it would be Fun setting around counting all the Money But after a While you would want to Do something Maybe Help others I want to Build Custom Built Environmental Quality Homes, Completely Off the Grid with our Own Power Solar,Windmill and,Water Treatment Plants etc. I just became a Good Motivational Speaker Instead Maybe You can Help Me Get this General Contractor Development Project off the Ground What do You Think?" "Yes " He Replied "I am Very Interested" "Then Think about it and I will Get Back with You, see You Later"   I hope this will be the last book I wrote. I said that last time thinking We said all I needed to say then I have these crazy dreams and the spirit Tells me more stuff. In My Dream world if I am seeing ,Hearing and touching things then did I leave my Fingerprint there? I know I asked this before but I want you to think about this Millions, Billions, trillions of different people thru out the World in this Lifetime so Imagine the last two three Thousand years how many different people all Here for a Different Reason going down a Different path why? Were are you Going? Were Have You Been? Have You Experience everything you want to? Did You Leave your fingerprint there? People Talk about the Tombstone they want on their Grave site they Put their Name, the Date they were Born and the date they Died sometimes the Only thing between these two dates is the Dash,People say What is your dash? What did You Accomplish during this Lifetime? Did you Leave your Fingerprint? When you Stand before this Creator on your Judgement day How will He Recognize you from the Million, Billion, trillion others out there? He created this Fingerprint, He Knows the Hair on your Head. You See People in every Life going thru Disease, Sickness ,Cancer, Handicap, rich, poor, all walks of life all Cultures, all languages some because they did some bad things in their Previous life others because they Chose to Experience these things. what do you need to Experience? This Lifetime I learned a little about Patience and Perserverance i was always in a Hurry,Why? I wanted to Accomplish so Much in a Short time. Now I am More Relaxed, if I do Not get to see the seven Wonders in this Lifetime then I will Make it a Priority to add it to my Bucket List in My Next Lifetime. One of my books I titled it the 13th Warrior because Jesus Christ had 12 Disciples and He was the 13th Teacher, which a lot of people want to say 13 is bad luck but actually Jesus had a Lot more followers the Bible only Mention those who wrote Books and were Real Close to Him, Remember there was no Television or Camera's No Microphones computers Telephones or Modern Technology so everything was handed down word of Mouth and you know if you tell ten People the same story, then by the time it gets down to the end then something is different, yes we have the Dead Sea Scrolls, the Nad Hammadi, the Forgotten Books and Many other Text, not Mentioned our Leaders Just picked out what they wanted you to read, they took the Female out of the Creation Process, Hid Her, and made a Dominant 3 Male Trinity Religion, Not Just Christianity but Buddah Islam Jewish and Other Religions decided to Hide the Female and If you did Worship Her then you were labeled as a Witch or pagan and Burned at a Stake ." Short break End of Chapter 13

Chapter Fourteen
scene Fourteen act Fourteen:
The Other Wheelbarrel

Everyone is Ready The Old man Speaks: "another Story or what you want to call a Secret, talks about a Crazy Man in a Insane Asylum, The Nurse asked Him What he Would Like for Christmas and He said, I Want a Wheel Barrel, What On Earth Would you Do with a Wheel Barrel? she said laughing? I Would Go around and Ask Everyones Problems and Put all Their problems in the Wheel Barrel, So All The Nurses Chipped in and Bought Him a Shiny, New, Red, Wheel Barrel. One Day the Nurse came to Work, to See the Guy Dragging The Wheel Barrel Upside down, She walked Up to Him and asked What Happened, He said I Went To Everybody and asked Them all Their Problems and The Wheel Barrel Got so Heavy, I Could Not Push it anymore.. She Thought for a Moment and said, What If You Get a Imaginary Shovel and Dig a Imaginary Hole and Bury all these Peoples Problems? Smiling, He said That Would Work. So we all Have Excess Baggage and Sometimes we Need to Put all Our Problems in a Imaginary Wheel Barrel and Dig a Imaginary Hole with a Imaginary Shovel and Put all Our Problems in the Hole, Bury them and Forget were We Buried Them. But our Male Chauvenistic Attitude that we are Man with Big Balls and Testosterone, so we are the Rulers,Is it our Ego? Our Pride? Our Vanity? 2,000 Years later have we,as a Society, and as Different Cultures Learned Anything?" I feel the Presence of the Ghost Camera "She is still Here, constantly filming my every Move, Yes even when I go to the bathroom I feel her Presence. I realize She Is my Guardian Angel, sent to constantly watch over me. she is Filming everything to document before our Creators everything.

Remember When someone told you they felt their Whole Life Flash before you at that moment? This is actually What is Happening. I read this Book called Wisdoms and the First Wisdom Was called Duality ,the Symbol for Duality is a Coin showing there are Two sides to everything, Good and Evil, Left and Right, Up and Down, forward and Reverse so If you Look at your Life you can use that Wisdom to Make you a better Person, You Now Realize you do have Good and Evil Inside of you, Its a Percentage Just like If you Are a Male During this life then you would have the male Hormone Testosterone Inside of You, but you would also have a Little of the female Hormone called Estrogen Inside You also. Scientist and Doctors have Proven this. I would Like to Think of when I was Young and the School Teacher was trying to teach us Fractions, She would Draw this Big Circle on the Board and say this is a Big Pie, so If You Cut this Big Pie In Half then you have this Line drawn thru the Middle, showing Now you Have Two Halves of a Pie, so two halves Equal a Whole. This is simple Teaching that a Child Had to Learn. They both had the Male Hormone Testosterone and Estrogen Inside of them. Now I want to Talk a Moment about these Hormones. A Long Time ago When I was In the Baptist, Christian Religion, I was Taught that Being Gay or a Lesbian was a Sin a Abmomination against the Bible Teaching. Everyone has read the Bible story about Sodom and Gomorrah. I was Taught If you go to a Bathroom, Pull Your Clothes off and Look down and you see a Man, then You Need to act like a Man,That is What you are during this Particular lifetime. Now we have the Hormones we can add, if needed but these is Only the Physical side of Us, Everyone Knows there are three sides to every Individual, Physical, Mental and Spiritual. I can see How Some People, Maybe a Female, in a Past Life and Having a Total Recall of that person and Carry-ing over some of these Emotions, Feelings and Baggage. i Know a Lot of gay People who Tell me they are a Woman Trapped in this Mans Body. Change-ing your Hormone By Adding the Steroid Testosterone will Help Physically but Mentally they still Believe they are still a Woman. We Know the Female Has the same Problem Thinking they are a male trapped in this Womans Body again now you are a Female in this Life, Get some Estrogen, Forget your past life, Enjoy Being a Female in this life and Experience what you need to Experience as a Female, maybe in Your Next Life you get to ne a male or What ever you want but do Not Play God and Look down and not be Happy with what you are today. God Does Not Make Mistakes, God made you a Female or a Male For a Reason, You Need to Experience these and Not Create some diseases because mentally you Remember What you are in a Past life forget all the Past Life Drama, You are a Male Now act Like a Male, You are a Female Now, Act like a Female. Physically add Hormones,

Mentally Seek Counseling, Spiritually Be the Person God/ Goddess created, Enjoy each Life to the Fullest. Why are you a Male In One Life and a Female in another life anyway? Why Can't you just be the same Life after life? Then How do You Experience Different Things if you are a Cookie cutter, life after Life, would the World be Pretty Boring If You Knew Exactly What you are going to do in each Life after Life after Life? Being Gay or a Lesbian is not a New thing, our Societies and Different Cultures have been Dealing with this Situation since the beginning. What is the Answer? Just like a Pack of Wolves they Have a Alpha Wolf or Alpha Dog which is the Biggest, Baddest Meanest Dog is the Alpha Dog and that is the Leader, so Goliath was Obvious the Alpha Dog, Right? Sometimes in our Society, Our Culture we have a Alpha Dog as Our Leader He Needs to be the Biggest, Baddest, meanest Person around and He Gets to be the King, Right? You Have to Obey the King, He can't Be some Whiney Wimpy Kid Ruling a Great nation But that was what David was. He Picked up a Little rock and Hit Goliath in the Only Vulnerable spot right Between the Eyes. All Of His Armor did Him no Good, Everyone has their Achilles Heel, their Vulnerable spot. What is your Weakness? Lucifer knows. He is the God of this World. He Is the First Born Son of this God and Goddess, Yes Jesus was a Important person. Just Like Hercules was Born Half man Half God so too was Jesus Born Half Male and Half God to Do Away with this Sacrificial law and To Teach you the truth.. Duality Teaches the Wisdom that Inside us, If you take that Pie and Cut it in Half then Cut each Half into Half then you have one fourth times four so Inside of you Now You have this duality of Good as Being three Fourths and Evil as only One Fourth. If You are Created during this Lifetime as a male species then you have three Fourth Make Hormone called Testosterone and One fourth Hormone called Estrogen Inside of you. This is Normal. You Can Not go to a Doctor or Surgeon and tell Him to use this Fancy Laser Surgery and remove this Evil Out of You or remove this Female Hormone Out of You. It can Not happen. We Have Figured this Hormone Thing out and Now we Can Take a Hormone Substitue and Change our Balance which is What some Weight Lifters and Body Builders do so they are Changing their Hormone Balance with Steroids and we Do Not Know what the Long term affect will be. We also Found this Hormone called Human Growth Hormone and we Figured Out we can Put his into Our Cattle, Chickens and Other Food supply to Make them Stronger and Better and Now We are eating this and Changing our Hormone Levels You can see 12 Year old Girls Developing breast and Young Boys being developed before their Time, we Do Not Know the Long term affect on this will Be, we are Playing God and Creating Sperm and Egg thru Artificial Insemination and we Will Eventually Think we are a God of some

Kind. Lucifer and all His Cohorts are Just setting back Laughing their Butts off at the Silly Humans Trying to Be Gods. We Steal From Our Mother Earth, Dig Holes in Her, and steal Her Diamonds, Emerald, Gold, Silver, Oil and gas and Think It Belongs to You. We Do Not realize we came Into this world naked, and with Nothing, and we will Leave this World naked and with Nothing, all the Material Things, we Think we own, will Not Buy us a Extra Moment Here on this Earth. We see Tornados , Earth-quakes,Tsunami, Lightning, Rain, Thunderstorms, Hurricanes etc" Lunch break again End of Chapter 14

Chapter Fifteen
King of the Mountain
Scene Fifteen Act Fifteen

" I Remember When I was a Kid we Had this Gravel Pit Close to Our Home, so all the Kids would Go over there on Weekends, when Everyone were Off Work and Climb on top of the Sand Pile. Once You Climbed on top You Could see all Over the Neighborhood. Things Looked Different when You are on Top of The Mountain. As a Kid, Full Of Energy You would Holler Out Loud, I am the King of this Mountain and You Would Dare Anyone to Take it from you. Of Course It Depends on How Many Other Kids were There and They Would Climb up the Mountain But You Had the Advantage, You were already Up there so It was Easy To Push Them back down The Only Rule was Once You Fell Down with Either Knee Touching the Ground you had to Give Up for that Day,Now Tomorrow You Could Come back and Challenge again. I Got to Stay Up on top of the Mountain for a While, Eventually I got Tired and after Wrestling with three Guys, the Fourth one who came up grabbed My Legs, Surprised at the new Maneuver I was Off Balance. Now I know the Basic Karate Stanch and that is Balance one Foot in Front of the Other Foot Behind at a Angle to Keep you Balanced. But after a While your Energy will Go Out, so I Tumbled down the Mountain along with My Pride. I mentioned this before in several books we have the N.A.A.C.P which is a great organization for colored People. Is this Equality? No, Only certain color of People can join plus they have Membership fee's and other Restrictions I want to Open a Worldwide Association for the Advancement of All People We can call it W.A.A.A.P there is No Membership fee's, No Restrictions No Religious Preference,No Culture Barrier and its Free to everyone. All you have to believe to Join is that its a World wide Association not just a National Association, for the Advancement of ALL People.instead of a Regular handshake shaking each others hand you reach beyond to the wrist and grab it and each person agree's this is the True Brotherhood hand shake of course our Sisters are Equal too and you shake their hand with the hand grabbing the Wrist showing YOU accept them as Equal,Not one being Superior to the other but Equal. What would the World be like if everyone reached out and gave the Brotherhood handshake and accept their Fellow Brother and Sister as Equal? Would the World be a Better place to Live? Would there be less Wars? Less Fighting? Its free Its Up to you to share with your Friends, Family and Neighbors the only way W.A.A.A.P. can be created is if Millions of People accept this as a start to Equality. Now I want to Talk about The Title of this Book one more time Shades of Red for thousands of years we hid the Female side of God,yes I call her the wife of God. Finally we, as a Society, are finally getting this Equality in everything but Religion. If you stop and think does having a Male Dominant Creator Make sense? All we know is what we were Taught. They can only Teach you what they were Taught. Slowly Religion is Changing,Yes we Now Don't Burn you at a Stake if you Honor the Goddess but we are still not Equal. A Day will come when the Goddess will Come back in all Her Glory. Some say She has always been here, for Those who understand, Respect and Pray to Her.Just Like our Male Creator God Has Many Names, so does His Wife. Who is right? who is Wrong? who gets to decide? I believe the Chosen People were the Hebrew, Not the Uncircumsised Jewish but the True Hebrew, so to me the Name for our Male Dominant Creator God would Be Yahweh and His Wife would Be Shekhinah,Again that is Only my Opinion,My "Version" what ever Name feels right for you Its not my job to Judge you one way or another Equality does Make sense It does not matter what Religion, What Skin color,What Language,What Custom or What Culture you were brought up to Believe in. Can we Have Equality? its up to you read this book tell others Would the World be a Better place if fifty Million People read my books? not because I wrote them but maybe because they make sense. I want to make it very Clear. Yes Jesus Christ, Lazarus and others were Resurrected. To me that Means they Kept the Same Body,the Same hair, Same Eyes, same Skin, the same Dna, the same Fingerprints. Now the Question is If you are Re-Incarnated and Have a New Body,a New Skin color, New Hair color, New Eye color but have the same Spirit/Soul could you still Have the same Fingerprints? When someone dies, Society just removes the Fingerprint from its Computer base, Maybe a Day will come when Religion will be Upgraded to were it needs to be and Society will keep these Finger-prints on a Archive Computer base and see what happens Twenty years from now. Its a matter of time, If enough People read this book and imagines that maybe I am Right then the Majority of this World will Realize the Difference

Between Resurrection and Re-Incarnation. Your Physical, Mortal Flesh and blood Human Body Does Die, Yes so does Your Spirit/Soul Just lay in the Ground? Could you be Judged and Go into a New Re-Incarnated Body, Why? Can You really Experience all the Things you Need to Experience in Only one Life? I hope my Definitions make sense to you its Not Just My Definition there are a Lot of People who Deep Down Believe this way,Remember all I know is What I was Taught, All You Know is what you were Taught. There is Good and Evil Inside of You Which one Is the Strongest? The One You Feed the Most. If you feed Evil,then You Become Evil,If you feed good then You Become good,Its Not Rocket Science its Normal Everyday Living life 101 Enjoy this Life Be somebody. Its Not Just Martin Luther King Who said it, But You to Can Say it. I am Somebody ,I may Not Be Rich But i am Somebody. I may be Black or White But I am Somebody. God and the Goddess Created You, In their Image, in the Image of Us, You Have a Unique Fingerprint, No one else has that so, Yes You are somebody. Are you Ready to Become the 13th Warrior? Avalon Church Ministry needs Warriors all over the World, In every City, every town to Help teach society the truths.Is this the Truth? What part of What I am saying is True? What part of What I am sayng Not True? All You Know is what you were taught, Your Sub-conscious will Only Accept what you tell it to believe in,They Can Only Teach you what they were Taught and Their Sub-conscious will Only Accept what they Tell it to Believe in, Who Is Right? Who Is Wrong Who Gets to Decide? this book is titled when God was a Woman, If you are a Pagan or into Wicca you would accept that Ideology but to me I teach Equality Yes there is a Male God and a Female Goddess as Equal. Does it matter if the Male was first or the female first? What matters to me is it takes both so we can say we have a Religion with a Male Dominant Creator or a Female Dominant Creator or we can wake up and Realize it does take both to make a Creation so to me I teach Equality. My e-mail is my name melvinabercrombie66@gmail.com, if you Have read this and want to Help Build a Avalon Church Ministry in your area, Let me know, I can help you set It up. What would the World Be Like If we Read this book and decided to help create this Equality? Would the World be a Better place if we had a Avalon Church Ministry In Every Town,Every City Every State and all Over The World? Would the World Be a better place, if Millions of people Read My Books and Understood these Equality Principles? Not because I wrote them, I am No Body, Just a Crazy Rebel Teacher, Trying to Teach People His Version of the Truth.Now You Know all The Elusive Treasures without Rubbing the Aladdin lamp But Do you get the One Wish? Do You Now Have this Understanding Heart? " Yes I Am Immortal This Book Is All About Immortality It Is Up to You To Wake Up and

Realize maybe You To Have a Immortal Spirit/Soul., Is Grandma Up In Heaven With Jesus Christ Right Now Or Is She Still In the Ground Waiting on this Future Rapture to Come? Neither. She Has Lived this Life, She Has Experienced What She Needed to Experience, Yes Her Temporary Flesh and Blood Mortal Body Did Die and Yes, She was Your Grandmother During this Lifetime, She Needed to Experience Being a Grandmother and You Needed to Experience Her as Your Grandmother. She Has Been Judged and Probably In another Life. Now You Understand Why Some People go thru a Life With Certain Disease's, Certain Illness or Handicap, Blind,Etc. You Can Not Experience Everything you Need to Experience In Only One Lifetime. Its Impossible to Experience Everything you need to Experience in a Hundred Lifetimes You Have a Right to Ask Questions and Demand Answers, Send Me a E-mail, Read this Book Over and Over again, You Are Here to Experience You Could have a Immortal Spirit/Soul Only You Can Answer That Question, Tell all Your Friends the Shades of Red and see if You can come up with More or less, Yes we can say 50 shades of red or Hundred Shades of red but we need to realize that our God did create Everything, so that means God, the Father did Create this Evil and you the reader can say there are a Hundred, Five Hundred, or a Thousand shades of red. We are all created Different, with different reasons for being here during this lifetime. My Shades of Red and My Elusive Treasure's, They are to Be Shared, they are Free, You Paid the Price of the Book or movie so Let Others Read it. Originally I Wrote this Book with Five Secrets Being of a Religious Nature and I used Only Five of these you are Currently Reading.Now I realized there are Many more Secrets so if you see Ten or twelve or only nine that is what you need to see at this time, some are ready to see fifteen others are not at that step yet so they see only eight thats ok when you are ready they will appear Trust God and ask for that Under-standing Heart. Be ready. If You Go to Amazon Books and Type in My Name, Melvin Abercrombie You will see Most of My Books are of a Religious Nature. To Me, The World is Not Following the Ten Laws. I wanted to Finally Make a Book with A Goddess as the second Secret Reincarnation Resurrection? as the third secret, the Kosher Food law as Number four Keeping the True 7th day Saturday sabbath as the Fith and Six teaching the Real Yeshua Ha Mashiach some were in there I would throw in the Fact you are Not saved by Grace but are Accountable maybe another Doctrine? so If you add all this to call this Olde Religion Wicca then you can understand were all this is going I am Not Creating a New Religion I am Not the Anti-Christ, I love Jesus Christ He is My Lord and Saviour I accept His Teachings. Why did the Church Kill him? They Knew He was telling Many Secret's,I like to call them Elusive Treasure's and They had to Kill Him to Silence Him,Now over 2,000 Years later we are still Scattered and Confused What ever name you want to call the Worship of a Male God and a Female Goddess as equal is up to You I Choose to Use the Name Avalon Church Ministry and You can Use this name in your area Let Me Know, I can Help you set it Up, you have My E-mail so Now Its up to you. I wamt Avalon Ministry to not only be a One day of the week Church Ministry, I have this Dream about getting Old useless Bottom Land,it seems every Town or city always has a Area that when it rains its under water and no one wants to buy this useless bottom land because it would cost to much to develop it.. So If you are a Non Profit organization then Imagine the County or city giving you this land for free under the Stipulation you will clear and bulldoze and Clean up the Useless property and Make it into a Taxable area were you could build Homes Business and other things. say there is two Hundred acres of Bottom land so you get Bulldozers clear out some of the Dead trees etc. You survey the land to find the Lowest point area and you build a Fifty acre Lake,as you dig down twenty thirty foot deep you move this dirt to the other area and build it up when it rains the water will naturally go to the Lowest Point so the lake you are creating the water will go there yes it will take time and Money You can build Windmills and Solar panels and Create a Off the Grid Power plant and with the Aerobic Sewer System, Create your own sewer plant by creating your own Lake you create your own water Treatment plant so you do not have to depend on what ever city or county you live in, you are completely self sufficent Now you build partial underground homes using Mother Earth as the Insulations Concrete and Steel yes, very little wood, Save as many Trees as Possible building water front and water view Property and a Few Commercial Retail stores. Any big Project of Two hundred acres has to figure the Price of the Land as part of the total Selling price being the Land had no cost the Initial cost of Backhoe, Bull dozer and Front end loaders would equal the price of Buying the Land Now building a Fifty Acre Lake what do you do with all that Dirt you take out? Believe me building a Lake twenty to thirty feet deep is a lot of Dirt but remember you are already under the water level and when it rains the water will naturally flow to the lowest point and Water front and water view Property is always in More demand then just regular ho hum development lots, Now can Avalon Church Ministry be a Tax Exempt Entity? Yes, Can We use the name Avalon as a Tax Exempt Development Company? I do not Know that will be up to Lawyers and each City to decide if we follow the Internal Revenue Tax Laws, Hire People to Run these Back hoe Bulldozer and File as a Non Profit Organization, then it is Possible but even if we have to say Avalon Church Ministry is one Entity and Avalon Development or Avalon Construction is another entity then the Point is, we are Taking Useless Bottom Land that for Hundreds of Years No one wants. We have a Meeting with the City or County involved and ask for a Proposal to take this useless land, Make it into a workable Development off the Grid maybe have power as a Optional standby and create Local Jobs, Create a Useless land into a Multiple Family Housing development maybe even a Apartment, Our Church Facility and other Retail space which Now can be a Taxable Item to help their city, they in return Provide Police, Fire and any other Services we agreed upon, Yes this will take Millions of Dollars. Anytime you build a Huge development with Water front and Water view Property then the Developer will have to build roads, Sidewalks, make this into a workable Development. What people would benefit from this, is a Off Grid ,Water front, water view, Custom Homes Created as you want them Yes Partial Underground to save Energy, cost less maintenance each home would be financed by the Avalon Corporation on a Fifteen or thirty year mortgage just like any othe Mortgage finance company. so everything will be created under Avalon, can you imagine building a development in every city every Town? Would that be so Bad? Yes We Honor our Creator God and the Female Goddess as Equal is that so Bad? you can still go to your Baptist,Methodist,Catholic, or what ever church you want to, is creating another Church so bad? Is Avalon meant for everyone? No of course not, there will always be different Religions, Different Beliefs, You put ten people in a Room, you may get 11 Different Opinions, Who is Right? Who is Wrong? Who Gets to Decide? Eventually people will figure out this off the Grid System is the way of the Future. Yes, Solar panels and Windmills is a Viable alternative Yes People will always choose Water front or water view Property over just ho hum boring lots. Yes, the cost of Building Customs unique homes will go up, can you save a Tree by using steel and Concrete? Wood is great, but termites, fire, warping, decay does happen yes, concrete will settle just like anything that is part of Mother Nature, so building a Perfect home is impossible, but building a Energy Efficient home custom built for you is possible, This is my dream, yes, it will take a lot of Money, Building a Church takes a lot of Money, buying two Hundred acres of Land and Building Custom Homes takes a Lot of Money, Creating Local Jobs, Creating Taxable Homes from Useless Bottom land and Making something that was a Eye sore into something Beautiful is that so Bad?? Shades of red is all about who you are why are you here? were are you Going? can there be a Hundred shades of Good? Can there be a Hundred Shades of Evil? can you come up with more or less? Just a Number? Only with Equality will we ever have Harmony and Balance United we Stand, Divided we Fall. Lucifer wants you to be Scattered and Confused, Now You Have My e-mail Address, You Know were My

Books are at,Amazon .com Only Thru People Buying My Books and Reading My Message will we Change the World, and I tried to Succeed, However I did Sneak a Little Religion here and There. I Hope You Will Take these Secrets, Shades of Red, or Elusive Treasure's What ever you want to Call them and Use Them. It does Not Matter What Religion, If any, you are Involved In. All You Know Is What you were Taught, All They Can Teach You Is What They Were Taught, Were You Live decides on who your Religion and or God is,You have No Choice, You were Born there, Now You have a Choice, listen to the People who Taught you what you know or go out and Search for who is right and Who is wrong, Some People Need to Experience A Life with Buddah others need to Experience the Krisna God of India, others need to Experience Various Christian Churchs and Religions, again who is right and Who is wrong? Who Gets to Decide? You do Now, I already said that Thank You For Now"........Amen and Shalom" Enough said the Old man has said all He wants to say, the Film crew take back to the office and delete some crazy film footage, try to make this into a one hour movie so what you are reading is the long version what you actually will see on the movie screen is a shorten version, I hope you got your seven dollars worth for buying this book, yes ask questions Help build a Avalon Ministry in your town its not about me its about all of you. Are you happy with the Religion you are in? then do not do anything, give this book to someone else, It takes millions of People to create the Baptist Organization ,Every city, every state, same as the Catholic or other so called Church Ministry.All I can do is plant a few seeds, Maybe you can help make these seeds into a Working Ministry were ever you live, Thank you End of Book

www.ingramcontent.com/pod-product-compliance
Ingram Content Group UK Ltd.
Pitfield, Milton Keynes, MK11 3LW, UK
UKHW051427170925
7945UKWH00034B/957

9 781974 502165